Intrusion Detection
A Machine Learning Approach

SERIES IN ELECTRICAL AND COMPUTER ENGINEERING

Editor: Wai-Kai Chen *(University of Illinois, Chicago, USA)*

Published:

SERIES IN ELECTRICAL AND COMPUTER ENGINEERING VOL. 3

Intrusion Detection

A Machine Learning Approach

Zhenwei Yu

University of Illinois, Chicago, USA

Jeffrey J.P. Tsai

Asia University, Taiwan
University of Illinois, Chicago, USA

Imperial College Press

ICP

Published by

Imperial College Press
57 Shelton Street
Covent Garden
London WC2H 9HE

Distributed by

World Scientific Publishing Co. Pte. Ltd.
5 Toh Tuck Link, Singapore 596224
USA office: 27 Warren Street, Suite 401-402, Hackensack, NJ 07601
UK office: 57 Shelton Street, Covent Garden, London WC2H 9HE

British Library Cataloguing-in-Publication Data
A catalogue record for this book is available from the British Library.

Series in Electrical and Computer Engineering — Vol. 3
INTRUSION DETECTION
A Machine Learning Approach

ISBN-13 978-1-84816-447-5
ISBN-10 1-84816-447-5

Printed in Singapore.

To our family

Preface

Networked computers reside at the heart of systems on which people now rely, both in critical national infrastructures and in private enterprises. Today, many of these systems are far too vulnerable to cyber attacks that can inhibit their functioning, corrupt important data, or expose private information. It is extremely important to make the system resistant to and tolerant of these cyber attacks.

An intrusion detection system (IDS) is a security layer to detect intrusions by monitoring and analyzing the events occurring in a computer system and network. Varied detection techniques on different audit data have been developed on its over 20 years history. However, two fundamental problems still have not been solved well: quantity and quality of the outputs (alarms or alerts) of the IDS. The problem on the quantity of alarms is that an IDS usually generates too many alarms which will overwhelm its user easily. Consequently, the alarms will be ignored by the operator, which make the IDS valueless. The second problem is that the performance will degrade because the normal behavior continuously changes and new attacks continuously emerge, i.e., the quality of alarms will degrade in two ways: miss alarms on true attacks and report too many false alarms on normal behavior.

Machine learning is the study of how to build computer programs that improve their performance through experience. Machine learning algorithms have proven to be of great practical value in a variety of application domains. They are particularly useful for: (a) poorly understood problem domains where little knowledge exists for the humans to develop effective algorithms; (b) domains where there are large databases containing valuable implicit regularities to be discovered; or (c) domains where programs must adapt to changing conditions. Not surprisingly, the field of cyber-based systems turns out to be a fertile ground where many security, reliability, performance, availability, and privacy tasks could be formulated as learning problems and approached in terms of learning algorithms.

This book introduces the basic concept and structure of an intrusion detection system. We discuss various attacks and countermeasures. We provide an overview of machine learning methods and give a classification of the existing work. Our focus is on the discussion of the application of machine learning technique in the development of an adaptive intrusion detection system. This book presents an automatically tuning intrusion detection system which adaptively controls the number of the alarms output to the system operator and tunes the detection model on the fly according to the feedback provided by the system operator when false alarms are identified. A hybrid detection model, which consists of profile for normal behavior and profiles for high level attack categories, is learned from training data to balance the detection accuracy and capability on new attacks. Experiments were performed on KDD'99 data set. The extension of this system for wireless sensor networks is also presented.

Finally, we would like to thank Steven Patt of Imperial College Press for his guidance of this project, and Han C.W. Hsiao and Peter T.Y. Tsai of Asia University for formatting of the book.

Zhenwei Yu and Jeffrey J.P. Tsai

Contents

Part A: Intrusion Detection for Wired Network

Part B: Intrusion Detection for Wireless Sensor Network

Chapter 1

Introduction

1.1. Background

Security concerns are becoming increasingly important in modern computer systems. With the development of networking and interoperation on public networks, the number as well as the severity of security threats has significantly increased quickly. In 2006, vulnerabilities were reported by Computer Emergency Response Team (CERT) almost every hour (Fig. 1.1) [1]. Although intrusion prevention techniques, such as user authorization/authentication (e.g., using password or biometrics), avoiding design/programming errors (e.g., clean room design), information protection (e.g., encryption) and firewall of network connection were developed and used to protect computer system, intrusion prevention alone is not sufficient because as system becomes more complex, there are always exploitable weaknesses in the systems due to design and programming errors, incorrect system configurations and operations, or various "socially engineered" penetration techniques. The policies that balance convenience versus strict control of a system and information access also make it impossible for an operational system to be completely secure. More systems deploy Intrusion Detection System (IDS) as another layer of security mechanism to protect the system. The term "intrusion" refers to attempts to compromise the confidentiality, integrity, availability of a resource, or to bypass the security mechanism of a computer or network system. An IDS tries to detect attempts to penetrate into a system by monitoring the events occurring in a computer system or network and analyzing them for signs of intrusions. It can generate and report alarms to system operators when it detects intrusive or abnormal activities. The history of intrusion detection can go back to 1980s, when James Anderson

1

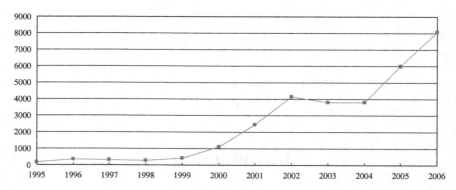

Fig. 1.1.   Statistics of vulnerabilities reported by CERT.

first proposed to monitor security threats through audit trails [2]. In its over 20 years history, varied audit data, including system activities, user activities and network activities have been used to detect intrusions. Different analysis/detection methods have been proposed and developed, from statistical analysis, expert system, model-based system, and machine learning or data mining-based system. Roughly, the detection methods can be classified into two board categories: misuse (signature based) detection and anomaly detection [3].

Misuse detection, characterizes a number of known attacks (misuse) to compromise a system and usually describes them as patterns/signatures. Misuse detection system monitors for the appearance of explicit patterns. As long as such a pattern is detected, an alarm will be reported to the operator. Such a system usually uses an expert system to identify intrusions based on a predetermined knowledge base. Recently, varied data mining techniques have been used to build such a pattern base automatically. Those systems have higher accuracy, but they could not detect any new intrusion without a pattern for the intrusion.

Anomaly detection is concerned with identifying events that appear to be anomalous with respect to normal system behavior. Profiles for normal user, system and network activity can be built. For an incoming activity, if no similar activity can be found on the profile, an alarm will be reported. Usually, the profile will be built using some statistic analysis techniques. Data mining techniques also have been used to build the profiles. Anomaly detection can identify new and previously unseen attacks. However, sometimes it is difficult to determine the boundary between acceptable and anomalous behavior at some time, so it will have higher false-positive rates. An experienced intruder could train such an intrusion detection system gradually to accept an intrusion as normal behavior.

1.2. Existing Problems

At present, two fundamental problems still have not been solved well: *quantity* and *quality* of the outputs (alarms or alerts) of the IDS. The problem on the quantity of alarms is that an IDS usually generates too many alarms which will overwhelm its system operator. Consequently, the alarms will be ignored by the operator, which make the IDS valueless. The second problem is that the performance will degrade because the normal behavior continuously changes and new attacks continuously emerge, i.e., the quality of alarms will degrade in two ways: miss alarms on true attacks and report too many false alarms on normal behavior. Missing alarms on true attacks is harmful to the monitored computer system. False alarms waste operator's time and reduce the operator's trust in the IDS. The alarms will be ignored by operator when the IDS is not trusted by the operator and make the IDS useless.

1.2.1. *Alarm management*

IDSs are designed to monitor computer system/network to report any suspected activity. The report can be made in different ways, such as sending an email, play some sounds, paging the system administrator or security officer, and so on. We call the report content on the name of alarms (both of term alarm and alert are used in IDS community for it), which include timestamp, possible attack type, and some other related information. The alarms are the outputs of an IDS. They are supposed to be valuable to system operator. We also believe that the system operator or analyst should take some actions to deal with the alarms. At least, the operator should make a decision on whether it reports a true intrusion or it is a false-positive alarm.

But an IDS could generate quite large amount of alarms at some certain period. The following message excerpted from a mail list which focus on intrusion detection could give a basic impress on how many alarms an IDS could report. "Usually, I will receive about 1,000 emails from my IDS every day, in each email, 8 alarms are included. ... I use the default signature base". "The signature profile must be tuned; otherwise, the alarms will be totally ignored within 2 weeks". Let us do a simple mathematic problem.

When the IDS reports 8,000 alarms every day, for a responsible system operator, how much time is allowed for him to analyze one alarm? The result is shown below.

$$\frac{24 \times 60 \times 60}{8,000} = 10.8 \text{ seconds.}$$

In most cases, it is too short to make the conclusion on whether it reports a true intrusion. In the above equation, we assume that there is one operator monitoring the alarms 24 hours a day. If there are not enough qualified system operators, things go worse.

The first problem is how to manage these alarms. It is a well-known problem existing in IDSs. Some research works have been done to overcome this problem. There are two board types of methods. The first one is to reduce the alarms, especially the false-positive that an IDS could generate, i.e., improve the analysis methods. The second method is to add another layer above the IDS, before the alarm reach the operator. In this layer, alarm can be filtered or some support information on analyzing the alarms can be generated to help the operator.

There are several available solutions to address the quantity problem, such as alarm correlation, alarm filter, and event classification. Alarm correlation provides support to analyze the alarms. However, the actual alarms are not reduced at all. Alarm filter and event classification process can reduce the false alarms, but do nothing to the true alarms. Sometimes, when the monitored system is under volume of attacks, even without any false alarm, the amount of true alarms could be quite large.

1.2.2. *Performance maintenance*

The value of an intrusion detection system is on the proper actions performed by the system user against the true intrusions. However, most of alarms usually are false alarms. The ratio of false alarms and true alarms in most commercial signature-based intrusion detection systems could vary from 5:1 to 20:1. New attacks leveraging newly discovered security vulnerabilities emerge quickly and frequently. The monitored system is always on the risk that it will be attacked by new attacks. The misuse detection methods are short of the capability to catch the new attack. The anomaly detection system (mainly are data mining-based system) relies on the quality of training data greatly. However, it is difficult to collect high quality training data, at least it is impossible to collect all related data on new attacks to train a detection model before those attacks are identified and understood. So anomaly detection systems usually have much higher false rate. In addition, due to new hardware and software deployed in the system, system and user behaviors will keep changing, which causes detection models to degrade in performance. As a consequence, a fixed detection model is not suitable for an intrusion detection system. Instead, after an IDS is deployed, its detection model has to be tuned continually.

The second problem is how to maintain the performance of the IDS. For commercial products (mainly signature/misuse-based IDS), the main tuning method is to filter out signatures to avoid generating noise and to add new signatures. However, the problem of such a solution is the timing. Usually, vulnerabilities are found by some users with particular interests other than the software provider. Their findings will be spread through underground network quickly. The new attack against the new vulnerability will emerge more quickly. Therefore, we cannot rely only on the system provider or the IDS provider to update them. In data mining-based intrusion detection, system parameters are adjusted to balance the detection rate and the false rate. Such tuning is coarse and the procedure must be performed manually by the system operator. In research project, adaptive learning and incremental mining were two efforts to solve this problem. Adaptive learning needs to train a special purpose model that forces the user to collect and construct high quality training data. Incrementally mining a new model in real time from unverified data incurs the risk that the model could be trained by an experienced intruder to accept abnormal data.

Machine learning is critical in the study of how to build computer programs that improve their performance through experience. Machine learning algorithms have proven to be of great practical value in a variety of application domains. They are particularly useful for: (a) poorly understood problem domains where little knowledge exists for the humans to develop effective algorithms; (b) domains where there are large databases containing valuable implicit regularities to be discovered; or (c) domains where programs must adapt to changing conditions. Not surprisingly, the field of intrusion detection turns out to be a fertile ground where many security, reliability, performance, and privacy tasks could be formulated as learning problems and approached in terms of learning algorithms.

This book discusses how machine learning being used in intrusion detection. Particularly, we present an Adaptive Automatically Tuning Intrusion Detection System (ADAT IDS) [113] to overcome the existing quantity and quality problems on the alarms. We build the system with one thing in mind, the intrusion detection system is a tool used by the operator. The tool should adjust itself to match the operator, rather than the operator adjusts himself to fit the tool. The ADAT IDS is expected to have two important properties: it should control the amount of alarms adaptively depending on the alarms' processing situation by the operator and tune its model automatically according to the feedback from the operator to maintain its performance.

We discuss the attacks and countermeasures of software systems in Chap. 2. Chapter 3 introduces machine learning methods. Chapter 4 presents the basic concept and structure of intrusion detection system (IDS). We then describe the work related to the quantity and quality problems of alarm management in Chap. 5. In Chap. 6, we propose solutions to these problems. Chapter 7 covers our system prototype and performance evaluation. We present the related work on intrusion detection system in wireless sensor network in Chap. 8. And propose our extension of the intrusion detection system to wireless sensor networks in Chap. 9. The conclusion and the future research work are in Chap. 10.

Chapter 2

Attacks and Countermeasures
in Computer Security

In this chapter, we provide an overview of general categories of attacks and countermeasures existing in computer security [7, 117].

2.1. General Security Objectives

It is helpful to identify security objectives before discussing various security problems in software systems. Different systems and applications have their own security objectives; while they share quite a few common ones. Generally speaking, a secure software system should meet the following security objectives, some of which are explained based on NIST definitions [4] in alphabetical order below.

2.1.1. *Accountability*

Accountability is the security goal that generates the requirement for actions of an entity to be traced uniquely to that entity. This objective requires that users and administrators will be held accountable for behavior that impacts the security of information. Accountability is often an organizational policy requirement and directly supports non-repudiation, deterrence, fault isolation, intrusion detection and prevention, and after-action recovery and legal action. This objective has more importance in electronic business. For example, a customer intends to buy a certain product from an online store. The user and the store have a session of communications, so that the user tells the store about his credit card to be charged, and the store gives the user a receipt. Both the user and the store should be accountable for their communications and behaviors.

2.1.2. *Assurance*

Assurance grounds for confidence that other security goals (including integrity, availability, confidentiality, and accountability) have been adequately met by a specific implementation. "Adequately met" includes (1) functionality that performs correctly, (2) sufficient protection against unintentional errors (by users or software), and (3) sufficient resistance to intentional penetration or by-pass.

2.1.3. *Authentication*

Authentication requires verifying the identity of a user, process, or device, often as a prerequisite to allowing access to resources in a system. This objective requires that the identity (or other relevant information) of an entity or the originator of data can be verified and assured. Satisfying this objective can prevent faking or masquerading from happening.

2.1.4. *Authorization*

Authorization is to grant or deny access rights to a user, program, or process. This objective requires that only legitimate users can have the rights to use certain services or to access certain resources, while unauthorized users are kept out. It is also called "access control". Authorization is often combined with authentication as the result of authentication is usually used to decide whether or not to grant a request of an entity. To achieve those security properties, digital signatures may be required in addition to password access.

2.1.5. *Availability*

Availability is the security goal that generates the requirement for protection against intentional or accidental attempts to perform unauthorized deletion of data, or to cause unavailability of service. This objective requires that data and system can be accessed by legitimate users within an appropriate period of time. Some attacks such as Denial of Service or instability of the system may cause loss of availability.

2.1.6. *Confidentiality*

Confidentiality is the security goal that generates the requirement for protection from intentional or accidental attempts to perform unauthorized data reads. Confidentiality covers data in storage, during processing, and while in transit. This objective requires that data should be protected from any unauthorized disclosure. That is to say, it should be ensured that data can only be read by persons or machines for which it is intended. A loss of confidentiality hurts the data privacy.

2.1.7. *Integrity*

Integrity can be classified into data integrity and system integrity. Data integrity is the objective that data should not be altered or destroyed in an unauthorized manner to maintain consistency. It also covers data in storage, during processing, and while in transit. System integrity is the objective that a system should be free from unauthorized manipulation when it performs its intended function in an unimpaired manner.

2.1.8. *Non-repudiation*

This objective requires that either side of a communication cannot deny the communication later. Important communication exchanges must be logged to prevent later denials by any party of a transaction. This objective also relies on authentication to record the identities of entities.

Besides the objectives mentioned above, more security objectives may be identified and required in different situations. Generally speaking, accountability, availability, assurance, confidentiality, and integrity are five main security objectives of a software system. These security objectives are not isolated. Instead, various relationships exist among them. Assurance is the base security objective that other objectives are built on. Confidentiality and integrity can affect and also be affected by each other. Based on them, availability and accountability can be achieved.

Figure 2.1 shows the relationships among these five main security objectives. For a specific system, certain security objectives may conflict to each other sometimes. For example, to increase the availability level, a system may have to compromise its confidentiality or integrity level. Therefore, an overall security policy is often preferred other than individual security objectives.

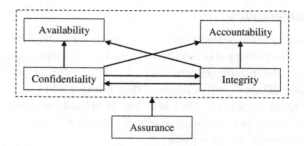

Fig. 2.1.   Relationship among five main security objectives.

2.2. Types of Attacks

It is desired that a software system can meet all security objectives. But many issues compromise the system security. The most severe issue is various attacks which take advantage of the weakness and vulnerability of a system, and try to breach the system. A lot of attacks have been noticed and tackled with, while more new attacks are hiding or arising. It is helpful to know how many types of attacks are there and what their characteristics are. Viewed from different aspects, attacks to a software system can be classified into different categories. In this chapter, we summarize and categorize types of attacks based on their negative effects on security objectives. Therefore, most existing attacks fall into three major categories: attacks against availability, attacks against confidentiality, and attacks against integrity. It should be note that these categories may be overlapping since quite a few attacks have multiple targets. Since this chapter is more from the technique point of view, certain attacks and threats which involve personal factors, such as social engineering threats, are ignored here.

2.2.1. *Attacks against availability*

Attacks against availability mainly attempt to overload available resources or make a particular facility unavailable at a certain time for the attackers' sake. Sometimes, such attacks may not totally disable targeted resources and services, but just degrade them. Attacks in this category are usually DOS (Denial of Service) attacks. According to CERT® Coordination Center [5], a DOS attack is characterized by an explicit attempt by attackers to prevent legitimate users from using system services, or cause delaying of time-critical operations. Time-critical may be milliseconds or hours, depending upon the service provided. Typically, DOS attacks can result in the unavailability of a particular network service or the temporary loss of all network connectivity and services. They can also destroy programming and files in a computer system. A commonly seen DOS attack on the Internet is simply to send more traffic to a network node than it is supposed to take, such that the functionality of that network node gets disabled. An example of such DOS attack is the smurf attack or a PING flood, in which a smurf attacker sends PING requests to an Internet broadcast address and spoofs the return address as the target victim's address. The victim's network line would be filled by these PING replies and its network service would be brought to its knees. SYN flood attack is another example of DOS attack using the similar strategy to PING flood.

DOS attacks come in a variety of forms and aim at a variety of services. Following are three basic modes of attacks:

(1) Consumption of scarce, limited, or non-renewable resources;
(2) Destruction or alteration of configuration information; and
(3) Physical destruction or alteration of network components.

DOS attacks usually occur intentionally and maliciously, but they can also happen accidentally. DOS attacks usually do not result in the theft of information or other security loss. However, these attacks can cost the target system significant time and money.

2.2.2. *Attacks against confidentiality*

Attacks against confidentiality mainly attempt to reveal the contents of communications, or leak sensitive data and information of a system. Attacks in this category have different forms, while the Eavesdrop attack is a primary class.

An Eavesdrop attack is an attack where communication is monitored to reveal the secret. It usually occurs when some wiretap devices are plugged into computer networks and Eavesdrop on the network traffic. Then a sniffing program lets someone listen to computer conversations. However, computer conversations consist of apparently random binary data. Therefore, network wiretap programs also come with a feature known as "protocol analysis", which allow them to decode the computer traffic and make sense of it.

Originally, the base for this type of attack is the shared principle on which the Ethernet is built, which is, all machines on a local network share the same wire. Therefore, all machines are able to "see" all the traffic on the same wire. Ethernet hardware is built with a filter that ignores all traffic that does not belong to it. A wiretap program turns off this filter, and put the Ethernet hardware into promiscuous mode. Later networks are developed from share mode to switch mode. Electronic eavesdropping, which applies electromagnetic devices such as a frequency analyzer and a tuned antenna, emerges as well. They are often taken advantage of by amateur eavesdroppers to perform eavesdrop attack. Eavesdrop attacks usually cost the loss of confidentiality and secrecy of a system, but do not hurt integrity.

Another form of attacks against confidentiality is data aggregation, which allows an attacker to deduce classified information from unclassified information. For example, an attacker may determine a specific employee's approximate salary by looking into the department's personnel expenditure before and after hiring this employee.

Password or encryption key sniffing also do harm to system confidentiality. This kind of attack enable an attacker gain unauthorized access to system or facilities by stealing legitimate users' passwords and masquerading as the legitimate user, or inspect encrypted files or communication messages by using encryption keys got illegally. This attack usually takes advantage of the "broadcast" technology used in most networks. When a legitimate user tries to log into a system remotely, or an entity of a communication tries to request an encryption key, the attacker's computer can get those secure information if the security of the network is not strong enough. It should be note that after a password or encryption key has been sniffed by an attacker, he/she can go ahead to perform certain attacks to hurt system integrity.

2.2.3. *Attacks against integrity*

Attacks against integrity mainly attempt to modify communication contents or data in a system. Attacks in this category also have many various forms.

One primary form is the Man-in-the-Middle (MITM) attack, which happens when an attacker sniffs packets from network, modifies them and inserts them back into the network. In MITM attack, an attacker is able to read and modify messages between two parties at his/her will, without letting either entity know that they have been attacked. MITM attacks remain a primary weakness of public-key-based system. The introduction of signed keys by a trusted third party can help with designing a mechanism for coping with such attacks.

Another form is the Web Site Defacing and Hijacking attack. This type of attack may modify, destroy, or replace some web pages of certain institutions. Visitors of those institutions are given altered information, or hijacked to other site without knowing the fact. Attackers can then request and collect certain information or gain benefits from the clients. Weaknesses of web server are always the base for this type of attacks.

Attacks on authentication usually hurt integrity as well. Such attacks generally allow an attacker to masquerade as a user with higher privilege than him/her. Password sniffing is used toward password-based authentication systems to perform attacks against confidentiality and integrity, while disclosure of encryption key is used toward cryptographic authentication systems. For the latter system, replay attack exists as well. A replay attack is an attack in which the attacker records data or communication contents and replays it later to deceive the recipient. For example, the initiator of a session Alice sends and receives several messages to and from the responder of this session Bob, while an intruder Elisa stores all the messages. After this session is over, Elisa may send the packages sent by Alice before to Bob again in order to impersonate as Alice in a new session. If Elisa succeeds, Bob is tricked to believe he has another session with Alice. Therefore Elisa can use Alice's privilege to access and modify information or resources of Bob.

2.2.4. *Attacks against miscellaneous security objectives*

Attacks are not always toward one single security objective. On the contrary, many of them have multiple security objectives as their attacking targets. Viruses, unauthorized access attacks, and code exploit attacks are to be introduced below as three examples in this category.

Viruses are self-propagating entities that move across the nodes of the Internet. The life cycle of a virus begins when it is created and ends when it is completely eradicated. Its complete life cycle contains the following stages: creation, replication, activation, discovery, assimilation, and eradication. It is not hard to understand the creation, replication, and eradication. So we will only explain the rest three stages in more details here. A virus with damage routine will be activated when certain conditions are met, for example, on a certain day or when the infected user performs a particular action. On the contrary, a virus without damage routine does not activate. Instead, they only cause damage by stealing storage space. The "discovery" stage usually follows activation, but not necessarily. When a virus is discovered, it is sent to certain organizations for documenting and to those antivirus software developers for analysis. Then antivirus software developers modify their software so that the software can detect or kill the new virus. This stage is called "assimilation". The ability to replicate is the unique characteristic of viruses. Another commonality is that they may contain a damage routine that delivers the virus payload toward system confidentiality and system integrity. Such payload may destroy files, reformat hard drive, or cause other damages. Even if a virus does not contain a damage routine, it can still degrade the overall performance of a system to its legitimate users by consuming storage space and memory, which hurt system availability.

Unauthorized access attacks include unauthorized use of resources and illicit access of data. An attacker may impersonate as a legal user or bypass the authorization procedure which is not designed very well. The "backdoor" may be used to perform such attack. A backdoor in a computer system is a method of bypassing normal authentication or obtaining remote access to a computer, while intended to remain hidden to inspection. The backdoor may take the form of an installed program or could be a modification to a legitimate program. This type of attack may hurt system and user confidentiality as well as their integrity.

No software system is perfect. Code exploit attacks exploit software flaws to gain control of a computer, or to cause it to operate in an unexpected manner. Such attacks often come in the form of Trojan horses, for example, non-executable media files which are disguised to function in the system. Code quality is a key point when code exploit attack is taken into consideration. Some development methodologies rely on testing to ensure the quality of any code released. But they often fail to discover extremely unusual potential exploits. According to the difference of software flaws being exploited, this kind of attack may do harm to system confidentiality, integrity, and availability.

2.3. Countermeasures of Attacks

In order to counter various attacks, a lot of methods have been designed and proposed. Although they cannot solve all problems, they increase the security level of a software system. A countermeasure does not necessarily aim at one single attack. On the contrary, many countermeasures can provide protection against multiple attacks. These countermeasures may be applied in different layers of a computer system, such as physical layer or network layer, operating system layer which includes file system management, database management layer, or application layer. In the following, we introduce some categories of countermeasures. They are high-level techniques, and there are various concrete techniques to implement them.

2.3.1. *Authentication*

When considered as a countermeasure of attacks, authentication refers to the process whereby one entity proves its identity to another entity. In many situations, authentication is the most primary security service on which other security services depend. Ensuring authentication plays an important role in reinforcing those security objectives of a software system, such as accountability, authorization, confidentiality, integrity, and non-repudiation. Authentication is also a powerful shield protecting a software system from attacks toward those security objectives. In most cases, authentication establishes the identity of a human user to a computer system and is called "user-computer authentication". In other cases, authentication is also needed between computers or processes in a distributed environment. These two types of authentication are to be introduced below [6].

(1) **User-Computer Authentication**

User-computer authentication is often done through checking of passwords, cryptographic token or smart card, or biometric features such as a fingerprint. Password-based authentication is the most common technique and has been widely used. But it is vulnerable to attacks since a password can be guessed and shared. It is desired that a user can choose his/her passwords intelligently and change the passwords regularly. Authentication using a cryptographic token or smart card is much stronger than using passwords, because the token or a smart card is a hardware device equipped with a cryptographic key. This key does not leave the hardware device. But the token or smart card can also be shared or stolen. Biometric authentication takes advantage of the fact that biometric features are different from person to person. It has been used for applications requiring high level security. But it is also vulnerable to replay attacks and it needs cumbersome equipments. Therefore, combination of these methods is really needed.

(2) **Authentication in Distributed Systems**

In a distributed system, authentication is required repeatedly when a user accesses multiple machines and uses multiple services. Typically a user logs into a workstation using his/her password and then the workstation connects to other computers in this system on the user's behalf. Authentication becomes more complicated in a distributed system. One reason is that some third party can fake as others by actively eavesdropping or wiretapping others' communications. Drawbacks in some communication protocols are also used by attackers to achieve this goal. Therefore, formal methods should be used to verify the correctness of those protocols before they are put into use [7].

Authentication is usually implemented using two methods, one of which is called "message authentication code", the other is called "digital signature". A message authentication code is a short and non-transferable signature on a document. It is specific to an entity and cannot be verified by other entities. So it cannot be transferred and therefore cannot be used for contracts or receipts, which need to be saved and verified in case of a conflict. But it can be used for entities to make sure that the message they obtain is from the entity they expect. A message authentication code requires that the sender and the receiver of the authenticated message both know a symmetric secret used to generate and verify the message authentication code. This secret can be produced by one of the participants, and sent over in an encrypted form to the other, using a public key encryption method. Message authentication codes can be implemented using stream ciphers, e.g., RC5. Since a message authentication code is very efficient, it is useful for individual, small messages in interactive protocols. A digital signature is an authentication on a document and is computed using the secret key or private key of the signer on the document. A signature can be verified by anyone using the public key of the signer, the document signed, and the signature on the document. Therefore, it can be transferred and useful for contracts, receipts, etc. A digital signature is usually long, e.g., 1,024 bits, and not very quick to produce and verify. For these reasons, digital signatures should only be used when message authentication codes cannot offer the required functionalities.

2.3.2. *Access control*

Access control is the collection of mechanisms that permits managers of a system to exercise a directing or restraining influence over the behaviors, usage, and contents of a system. It permits management to specify what users can do, which resources they can access, and what operations they can perform. This technique is also known as "authorization". It is quite essential in software system security, as it grounds for higher-level security objectives such as confidentiality and integrity. Appropriate access control may prevent a software system from certain attacks, such as unauthorized access attacks.

Since access control is the process of determining whether an identity (plus a set of attributes associated with that identity) is permitted to perform some action like accessing a resource; access control usually requires authentication as a prerequisite. Authentication and access control decisions can be made at different points by different organizations. But these two are not necessarily separated. A number of security products or protocols implement these two procedures together, such as the IEEE 802.1x. It is an open-standard-based protocol for authenticating network clients or ports on a user ID basis. It takes the RADIUS methodology and separates it into three distinct groups: the Supplicant, the Authenticator, and the Authentication Server. This protocol provides a means of restricting network access to authorized users.

It is necessary to make a distinction between access control policies and access control mechanisms. Policies are high level guidelines which determine how accesses are controlled and how access decisions are determined. Mechanisms are low level software and hardware functions which can be configured to implement a policy. Generally speaking, there are three access control policies [8].

(1) **Mandatory Access Control**

Mandatory access control (MAC) policy compares the sensitivity label at which the user is working to the sensitivity label of the object being accessed. If MAC checks are passed, the user is given the access rights on the object. If not, the access request will be refused. MAC is mandatory because the labeling of information happens automatically, and ordinary users cannot change labels unless they are authorized by an administrator.

When the security policy of a system has the following two requirements: (1) the protection decisions must not be decided by the object owner; and (2) the system must enforce the protection decisions, the need for a mandatory access control (MAC) mechanism arises. MAC policy is supported by POSIX.6 standard, which provides a labeling mechanism and a set of interfaces that can be used to determine access based on the MAC policy.

(2) **Discretionary Access Control**

Discretionary access control (DAC) is the most common type of access control policy implemented in computer systems today. It restricts access to objects based on the identity of users and/or groups to which they belong. DAC is discretionary since a user with certain access permission is capable of passing that permission to any other user directly or indirectly. DAC controls are used to restrict a user's access to protected objects on the system. The user may also be restricted to a subset of the possible access rights available for those protected objects. Access rights are the operations a user may perform on a particular objects, e.g., read, write, and execute. Since DAC restricts access to objects based solely on the identity of users who are trying to access them, the identities of both the users and objects are the key to DAC. In most systems, any program which runs on behalf of a user inherits the DAC access rights of that user. This basic principle of DAC contains a fundamental flaw that makes it vulnerable to Trojan horses. Since the DAC permissions on system objects, usually files, can only be changed by the administrator who owns them, DAC is often used along with MAC to control access to system files.

(3) **Role-Based Access Control**

Role-based access control (RBAC) is receiving increasing attention as a generalized approach to access control. In an RBAC model, roles represent functions granted within a given organization and authorizations. Authorizations granted to a role are strictly related to the data objects and resources that are needed by a user in order to exercise the functions of the role. Users are thus simply authorized to "play" the appropriate roles, by acquiring the roles' authorizations. When a user logs in a system using RBAC, she/he can activate a subset of the roles she/he is authorized to play. The use of roles has several well-recognized advantages. Because roles represent organizational functions, a role-based model can directly support security policies of the organization. Authorization administration is also greatly simplified. If a user moves to a new function within the organization, there is no need to revoke the authorizations she/he had in the previous function and then grant the authorizations he/she needs in the new function. The security administrator simply needs to revoke and grant the appropriate role membership. RBAC models have also been shown to be able to support multiple access control policies. In particular, by appropriately configuring a role system, an RBAC model can support MAC and DAC as well.

Different mechanisms are used to implement the access control policies introduced above, such as Access Control Lists (ACLs), capabilities, and authorization table, which are different methods to store the access matrix of a system [9]. An access matrix is a spreadsheet with columns as resources, rows as users, and items as access rights the user in the corresponding row has over the object in the corresponding column. It is the simplest framework for describing a protection system. We discuss these mechanisms as follows:

(1) **Access Control Lists (ACLs)**

ACLs correspond to storing the access matrix by columns. They are associated with system objects and contain entries specifying the access that individual users or groups of users have to these objects. Access control lists provide a straightforward way of granting or denying access for a specified user or groups of users to a particular object. An access control list is a table that tells a computer operating system which access rights users have over a particular system object, such as a file directory or an individual file. Each object has a security attribute that identifies its access control list. The list has an entry for each system user with access privileges. The most common privileges for a file include the ability to read, write, and execute if the file is executable. Microsoft Windows NT/2000, Novell's NetWare, Digital's OpenVMS, and Unix-based systems are among the operating systems that use access control lists. The list is implemented differently by each operating system.

(2) **Capabilities**

Capabilities correspond to storing the access matrix by rows. Therefore, they are associated with system users and contain entries specifying the access rights each individual user or each group of users has to the system objects. Capabilities provide a straightforward way of identifying what objects can be accessed by a user or a group and how they can be accessed. Capabilities encapsulate object identity. When a process presents a capability on behalf of a user, the operating system examines the capability to determine both the object and the corresponding access. The location of the object in memory is encapsulated in the capability. Similar to ACLs, capabilities also aim at directly providing the relationships between subjects (users, group of users, processes on behalf of users, etc.) and objects (files, etc.). For example, both of them can answer the following two questions. The first question is "Given a subject, what objects can it access and how?" The second question is "Given an object, what subjects can access it and how?" For the first question, capabilities are the simplest way to answer while ACLs require all objects to be scanned; however, for the second question, ACLs are the simplest way while capabilities require all subjects to be scanned.

(3) **Authorization Table**

Access table corresponds to storing the access matrix by items. It contains entries specifying which user or group of users has what access right to which object. Sorted on objects, it becomes to a set of ACLs; while sorted on subjects, it becomes a set of capabilities. Therefore, it has the advantages of both ACLs and capabilities, and is more flexible than the above two. It is particular helpful for the access control in systems with sparse access matrixes.

Besides the three mechanisms introduced above, certain other mechanisms exist as well, such as ring-based access control, locks and keys. Those access control mechanisms can be used to enforced system security objectives, such as availability, integrity or confidentiality, by limiting access between methods and resources to collections of users or programs. Various techniques are utilized to implement those mechanisms.

2.3.3. *Audit and intrusion detection*

Audit is a posterior review of practices and events versus standards for purposes of evaluation and control. There are two types of audit: compliance audit and event audit. The definitions for compliance audit are different in different glossaries. We apply the definition from the E-Commerce PKI CA Glossary here that a "compliance audit is a review and examination of system records and activities in order to test for adequacy of system controls, to ensure compliance with established policy and operational procedures, to detect breaches in security, and to recommend any indicated changes in control, policy and procedures". Compliance audit can be classified into three common types further, which are regulatory audit, internal audit, and certified public accountant audit. Since compliance audit involves lots of social factors other than security itself, we will not go into its details here. Event audit is the process of gathering information about events happened in a system and analyzing the information to discover attacks to this system and reason about their causes. Event audit requires registration or logging of user requests and activities for later examination. Audit data is recorded in an audit trail or audit log, which varies from system to system. The auditing process can be performed both off-line and on-line. We will discuss event audit further below.

One important concept in event audit is intrusion detection. Intrusion detection is the process of monitoring the events occurring in a computer system or network and analyzing them for signs of intrusions, which are defined as attempts to compromise the confidentiality, integrity, availability of a resource, or to bypass the security mechanisms of a computer or network. Intrusion detection systems (IDSs) determine if actions perform intrusions base on one or more intrusion models. A model classifies a sequence of states or actions, or a characterization of states or actions, as "good" (no intrusion) or "bad" (possible intrusions). Modern IDSs primarily employ three models: misuse model, anomaly model, and specification-based model.

Misuse detection characterizes a number of known attacks (misuse) to compromise a system and usually describes them as patterns or attack signatures, so the misuse detection is also called "signature-based intrusion detection". Misuse detection system monitors system events and is able to detect the explicit appearance or minor variations of known signatures. Misuse detection system requires a database of attack signatures and usually uses an expert system to identify intrusions based on a predetermined knowledge base. A misuse detection system has higher accuracy, but it could not detect any new intrusion without a pattern or signature. Therefore, later IDSs use adaptive methods such as neural networks and Petri Nets to improve their detection abilities. For example, Kumar and Spafford [10] have adapted colored Petri Nets to detect both attack signatures and the actions following previously unknown attacks in their system Intrusion Detection In Our Time (IDIOT).

Anomaly detection uses the assumption that unexpected behavior is evidence of an intrusion. It requires determining a baseline of normal behavior. Then it is concerned with identifying events that appear to be anomalous with respect to normal system behaviors and reports when the computed results do not match the expected measurements. An anomaly detection system may use statistical, neural network, or data mining methods of analysis. Three different statistical models are used, which are threshold metric, statistical moment, and Markov model. For example, the Next-generation Intrusion Detection Expert System (NIDES) developed by SRI contains a statistical dynamic anomaly detector [11]. Anomaly detection can identify new and previously unseen attacks. But it is difficult to determine the boundary between acceptable and anomalous behaviors at some time, so it will have higher false-negative and false-positive rates. And an experienced intruder could train an anomaly intrusion detection system gradually to accept an intrusion as normal behavior.

Specification-based detection determines whether or not a sequence of intrusions violates a specification of how a program or system should execute. If so, it reports a potential intrusion [12]. Since the specification here is for security purpose, only those programs that may change the protection state of the system need to be specified and checked. Different from the misuse detection and anomaly detection, specification detection relies on traces or sequences of events and captures legitimate behaviors, not attack behaviors. Since it specifies the formalization of what should happen, it can detect intrusions using unknown attacks with low false alarms. However, extra efforts are needed to locate and analyze any program that may cause security problems in the system. Specification-based intrusion detection is still in its infancy. Ko *et al.* [13] developed a specification-based intrusion detection system for the UNIX environment and applied it to monitoring program *rdist*. Uppuluri and Sekar [14] developed a declarative pattern language called Regular Expressions over Events (REE) and embedded REE into a rule-based language called Behavior Modeling Specification Language (BMSL), based on which they came up with a specification of a system and compiled the specification to produce a fast detection engine. Their experiences on 1999 Lincoln Labs offline evaluation data and 1999 AFRL online evaluation showed that this method could realize the promise of specification-based intrusion detection and was very effective.

2.3.4. *Extrusion detection*

Extrusion detection or outbound intrusion detection is a branch of intrusion detection aimed at developing mechanisms to identify successful and unsuccessful attempts to use the resources of a computer system to compromise other systems. Extrusion detection techniques focus primarily on the analysis of system activity and outbound traffic in order to detect malicious users, malware, or network traffic that may pose a threat to the security of neighboring systems. Two examples are explained below:

BINDER (Break-IN DEtectoR) is a host-based system that detects break-ins of new unknown malware on personal computers by capturing their extrusions [119]. BINDER focuses on fast automated mechanisms for detecting break-ins of new unknown malware after a break-in occurs, as a way of mitigating damage. As a complement to existing prevention schemes, the approach decreases the danger of information leak and protects computers and networks from more severe damage.

In [120], it proposes a combination method which integrates both misuse detection and anomaly detection and applies data mining techniques for automatically generating detection rules and selecting proper features. In this method, both user and system activities are first recorded as raw data, such as keyboard/mouse events, process events, file system events, network connection events, and network traffic events. These raw data will then be analyzed by data mining techniques, such as association rule analysis, frequency analysis, link analysis, sequence analysis, and classification analysis. After these analyses, detection rules and proper features will be automatically generated. Then the detection rules can be used to detect existing extrusions and the proper features can be used to build normal profiles and detect future possible extrusions.

2.3.5. *Cryptography*

Cryptography is the technique of data encryption and decryption. It is widely used for protection of secure-sensitive contents such as passwords, files, and mutual communication. When two entities need to talk or exchange some information, the initiator should encrypt the readable plain text into illegible cipher text. Then the cipher text is transmitted over the communication channel, which is most probably unsecured. When the receiver gets the cipher text, it decrypts it into readable plain text again. Figure 2.2 illustrates the cryptography process.

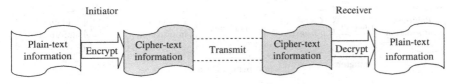

Fig. 2.2. Cryptography.

Encryption and decryption are based on certain algorithms and secrets, which are called "keys". It is desired that the choice of encrypt/decrypt algorithms and keys could satisfy the following requirements: encryption procedure is easy while any attempt to decrypt without the keys is difficult. According to the characteristics of keys, we can classify cryptography into two main categories: symmetric cryptography and asymmetric cryptography [7].

(1) **Symmetric Key Cryptography**

Symmetric key cryptography is also called "shared-key cryptography" or "single-key cryptography". As indicated by the name, this kind of cryptography uses a common key for both encryption and decryption. Besides the initiator and the receiver, a Key Distribution Center (KDC) is often needed. The KDC sends secret keys through secure channels to the initiator, who encrypts the clear text to cipher text using the keys. On the receiver side, cipher text is decrypted using the same secret keys sent by the KDC and becomes clear text. Figure 2.3 illustrates this process. A drawback of this kind of cryptography is that it requires large-scale distribution of the shared keys. In addition, although it can provide confidentiality of information, it provides little authentication. Neither does it validate the integrity of the data transmitted.

(2) **Asymmetric Cryptography**

Asymmetric cryptography is also called "public key cryptography". In this kind of cryptography, two mathematically linked keys are applied. If one of them is used to encrypt some information, the other key must be used to decrypt the corresponding cipher text. One of the two keys is kept secret by a certain entity and is referred to as the

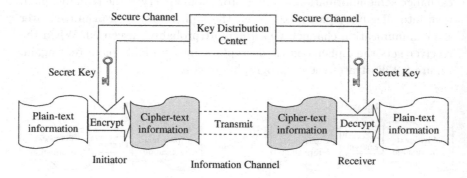

Fig. 2.3. Symmetric cryptography.

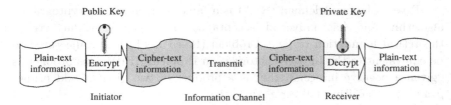

Fig. 2.4.   Asymmetric cryptography.

"private key" of this entity. This private key represents the identity of its owner. The second key, which is called the "public key", is made available to the public. For instance, if the initiator Alice wants to send a message to receiver Bob, Alice will use the public key of Bob to encrypt this message and then send the encrypted message to Bob. After Bob receives the encrypted message, he will decrypt it using his own private key. Since it is the assumption and requirement of asymmetric cryptography that it must be computationally infeasible to derive the private key from the public key, no one should be able to decrypt the message except for Bob. Therefore, asymmetric cryptography can provide authentication as well as confidentiality and integrity. Figure 2.4 illustrates the asymmetric cryptography.

(3) **Encryption/Decryption Algorithms**

Encryption and decryption algorithms are the foundation on which any cryptography technique is built. Therefore they are of great importance. Data Encryption Standard (DES) is a well-known symmetric key cryptography algorithm introduced in 1977 [5]. It encrypts data through confusion and diffusion. In this algorithm, blocks of 64 bits of data are encrypted and decrypted under the control of a 64-bit key. The encryption and decryption consist of 16 iterations; in each of which a separate key of 48 bits is used. The order in which the keys are used decides the process is an encryption or a decryption. Although DES has provided the impetus for many advances in the cryptography field and been the theoretical and practical groundwork for many other ciphers, it was broken in 1999. Its successor the Advanced Encryption Standard (AES) was proposed in 2001. The AES can use keys of 128, 192, or 256 bits and operates on blocks of 128 bits. It was specifically designed to withstand the attacks to which the DES showed weaknesses. At the same time, several other algorithms have been proposed to overcome the weaknesses in the DES, such as NewDES and IDEA.

Rivest Shamir Adelman (RSA) is a famous asymmetric cryptography algorithm and has universal acceptance. This algorithm has strong theoretical foundation of RSA Problem (RSAP), which is conjectured to be equivalent to the Integer Factorization Problem (IFP). This problem is "given a positive integer n that is a product of two distinct odd primes p and q, a positive integer e such that $gcd(e, (p-1)(q-1)) = 1$, and an integer c, find an m such that m^e is congruent to $c \pmod{n}$". No easy method has been found for the RSAP problem yet. RSA has been widely used because it can provide data and origin authentication and non-repudiation in addition to confidentiality. For instance, Alice encrypts her message using her private key. Anyone can read it with Alice's public key. However, no one can alter this message without being noticed because the altered cipher-text message cannot be decrypted correctly using Alice's public key. So if the message can be decrypted correctly, we can guarantee that this message is really encrypted by Alice based on the assumption that Alice is the only one who knows her private key and the corresponding public key bearing her name really belongs to her. RSA can also be used to provide both confidentiality and authentication simultaneously, which requires encryption with the sender's private key and the recipient's public key.

2.3.6. *Firewall*

A firewall is considered as the first line of defense in protecting private information. A firewall is a set of related programs or hardware devices, located at a network gateway server, which protects the resources of a private network from other networks users by allowing and disallowing certain types of access on the basis of a configured security policy. The term also implies the security policy that is used with the programs. Firewall technology provides both physical and logical protection between different networks. A firewall is often installed in front of the rest of the network so that all information flowing into this network has to be checked by this firewall and cannot get directly at private network resources. An enterprise with an intranet that allows its workers access to the Internet installs a firewall to prevent outsiders from accessing its own private data resources and for controlling what outside resources its own users have access to. Firewalls fall into three broad categories: packet filters, proxy servers, and stateful multilayer inspection firewalls [15].

(1) **Packet Filtering Firewalls**

Packet filtering is the most basic form of firewall security. In a packet filtering firewall, each packet is compared with a set of established rule sets first. Depending on the comparison results, the firewall can drop the packet, forward it, or send a message to the originator. Rules can include source and destination IP address, source, and destination port number and protocol used. So the header parts of packets often get examined. Packet filtering firewalls are usually part of a router firewall. A router is a device that receives packets from one network and forwards them to another. The advantage of packet filtering firewalls is their low cost and low impact on network performance. In addition, it has general and flexible structure, and provides extra security for the sub-network. Most routers support packet filtering.

Packet filtering firewalls only work at the network layer. Although they are fairly effective and transparent to users, it is difficult to configure them. In addition, large sets of rules can be difficult to manage. Therefore, packet filtering firewalls by themselves do not support sophisticated rule-based models and they are not adequate to secure a complex network from attacks. They are also susceptible to IP spoofing.

(2) **Proxy Servers**

A proxy server is a firewall component that acts as an intermediary between a LAN and the Internet. It monitors a session instead of examining each packet. Once a session is established, all packets in that session are allowed to cross. It can be classified into three categories according to its working layer: circuit-level gateway, application-level gateway, and stateful multilayer inspection firewalls.

Circuit-level gateways work at the session layer of the OSI model, or the TCP layer of TCP/IP. They monitor TCP handshaking between packets to determine whether a requested session is legitimate. Information passed to a remote computer through a circuit-level gateway appears to have originated from the gateway. This is useful for hiding information about the private network they protect. Circuit-level gateways are relatively inexpensive. Besides security features, a circuit-level gateway can also act as an intermediary providing transparency to its users. When a user proposes a request, the circuit-level gateway receives it first. If the request passes filtering requirements, the circuit-level gateway looks in its local cache of previously downloaded contents. If the desired page is found, the circuit-level gateway returns it to the user directly instead of forwarding the request to the Internet. If it is not found, the circuit-level gateway acts as a client on behalf of the user and requests the page from the server on the Internet. When the page is returned, the circuit-level gateway relates it to the original request and forwards it to the user. Therefore, an enterprise can ensure security, administrative control, and caching service by using a circuit-level gateway.

Application-level gateways can filter packets at the application layer of the OSI model and are application specific. Incoming or outgoing packets cannot access services for which there is no proxy. Because they examine packets at application layer, they can filter application-specific commands, which cannot be accomplished by either packet filtering firewalls or circuit-level gateways. Application-level gateways can also be used to log user activities and logins. They offer a high level of security, but have a significant impact on network performance because context switches slow down network access dramatically. They are not transparent to end uses and require manual configuration of each client computer.

(3) **Stateful Multilayer Inspection Firewalls**

Stateful multilayer inspection firewalls are a hybrid combination of the other types of firewalls. They operate primarily on the network layer of the OSI model and transparently to the end users. They examine certain key parts of a packet and compare them with contents in a database of trusted information. According to the comparison results, they allow the packet to go through or discard it. They allow direct connection between client and host, alleviating the problem caused by the lack of transparency of application level gateways. They rely on algorithms to recognize and process application layer data instead of running application specific proxies. Stateful multiplayer inspection firewalls offer a high level of security, good performance, and transparency to end users. However, they are expensive. In addition, if not administered by highly competent personnel, they are potentially less secure than simpler types of firewalls due to their complexity [15].

2.3.7. *Anti-virus software*

Anti-virus software is a class of software that looks for a virus or looks for indications of the presence of a virus in a data storage device, such as a hard drive, floppy disk, and CD-ROM and prevents these programs from performing their functions. Since new viruses are created and dispatched all the time, some antivirus software should be updated periodically. The market for antivirus software has expanded because of Internet growth and the increasing use of the Internet by businesses concerned about protecting their computer assets. It is desired that more than one antivirus software packages are installed in a system, since no single product can do everything. There are three main kinds of antivirus programs: scanners, monitors, and integrity checkers [16].

Currently, scanners are the most popular and the most widely used antivirus programs. They are programs that check for viruses by scanning the executable objects, such as executable files and boot sectors, for the presence of special code sequences or strings called "signatures". Each virus recognizable by scanners has a signature associated with it. Scanners mainly consist of a searching engine and a database of virus signatures. They are widely used because they are relatively easy to maintain and update. When a new virus appears, the authors of scanners just need to pick a good signature, which is present in each copy of the virus and at the same time is unlikely to be found in any legitimate program, and add the signature to the scanner's database. This is often done very quickly. In addition to scanning for virus signatures, some scanners go a step further. For instance, the "f-prot" from Frisk Software uses a heuristic analyzer to see if executable objects contain virus-like code, such as time-triggered events, and software load trapping. Heuristics is a relatively new, but effective way to find viruses without defined signatures yet. Scanning techniques have some other variations, like virus removal programs, resident scanners, virus identifiers, etc.

Monitors are memory resident programs, which continuously monitor computer's memory, automatically detect, and remove viruses without interrupting users' works. Once a program tries to use a function, which is considered to be dangerous and virus-like, the monitoring program intercepts it and either denies it completely or asks the user for confirmation. Unlike the scanners, the monitors are not virus-specific and therefore need not be constantly updated. But monitors have two main drawbacks which make them weaker than the scanners. One drawback is that monitors can be bypassed by the so-called "tunneling" viruses which attempt to follow the interrupt chain back down to the basic DOS or BIOS interrupt handlers and then install themselves. The other drawback is that monitors try to detect a virus by its behavior, which may cause many false alarms since viruses may use functions similar to those used by the normal programs.

Integrity checkers are programs which read the entire disk, compute some kind of checksum of the executable code in a computer system, and store the checksum in a database. The integrity checkers re-compute the checksum periodically and compare it with the stored original value to detect whether the executable code in this system has been modified. There are three main kinds of integrity checkers. The most widely used one is the off-line integrity checker, which checks the integrity of all the executable code in a computer system. Another kind is the integrity module. It can be attached to an executable file, which can check its integrity when starting its execution. The third kind is the integrity shell. It is a resident program which checks the integrity of an object only when this object is about to be executed. Integrity checkers are not virus-specific and do not need constant updating like the scanners. Currently, they are the most cost-effective and sound line of defense against the computer viruses. However, integrity checkers can only detect and report viruses, but cannot block them from infecting other files or systems. They usually cannot determine the source of infection either. Since the original checksum is considered to be the correct one for later comparison, integrity checkers must be initially installed in a virus-free system. In addition, they are prone to false-positive alerts since changes they detected may be legitimate changes of a certain program. Although integrity checkers have those drawbacks mentioned above, their future is predicted as bright by specialists [16].

Chapter 3

Machine Learning Methods

3.1. Background

Machine learning is concerned with the design and development of algorithms and techniques that allow computer systems to autonomously acquire and integrate knowledge to continuously improve them to finish their tasks efficiently and effectively. Machine learning algorithms have proven to be of great practical value in a variety of application domains. Not surprisingly, the field of intrusion/extrusion detection turns out to be a fertile ground where many security-related problems could be formulated as learning problems and approached in terms of learning algorithms. In this chapter, we will introduce machine learning techniques which could be used in intrusion detection systems [114–116].

3.2. Concept Learning

In concept learning, a target function is represented as a conjunction of constraints on attributes. The hypothesis space H consists of a lattice of possible conjunctions of attribute constraints for a given problem domain. A least-commitment search strategy is adopted to eliminate hypotheses in H that are not consistent with the training set D. This will result in a structure called the version space, the subset of hypotheses that are consistent with the training data. The algorithm, called the candidate elimination, utilizes the generalization and specialization operations to produce the version space with regard to H and D. It relies on a language (or restriction) bias that states that the target function is contained in H.

31

This is an eager and supervised learning method. It is not robust to noise in data and does not have support for prior knowledge accommodation.

3.3. Decision Tree

In decision tree learning, a target function is defined as a decision tree. Search in decision tree learning is often guided by an entropy based information gain measure that indicates how much information a test on an attribute yields. Learning algorithms often have a bias for small trees. It is an eager, supervised, and unstable learning method, and is susceptible to noisy data, a cause for overfitting. It cannot accommodate prior knowledge during the learning process. However, it scales up well with large data in several different ways.

3.4. Neural Networks

In neural network learning, given a fixed network structure, learning a target function amounts to finding weights for the network such that the network outputs are the same as (or within an acceptable range of) the expected outcomes as specified in the training data. A vector of weights in essence defines a target function. This makes the target function very difficult for human to read and interpret. This is an eager, supervised, and unstable learning approach and cannot accommodate prior knowledge. A popular algorithm for feed-forward networks is Backpropagation, which adopts a gradient descent search and sanctions an inductive bias of smooth interpolation between data points.

3.5. Bayesian Learning

Bayesian learning offers a probabilistic approach to inference, which is based on the assumption that the quantities of interest are dictated by probability distributions, and that optimal decisions or classifications can be reached by reasoning about these probabilities along with observed data. Bayesian learning methods can be divided into two groups based on the outcome of the learner: the ones that produce the most probable hypothesis given the training data, and the ones that produce the most probable classification of a new instance given the training data. A target function is thus explicitly represented in the first group, but implicitly defined in the second group. One of the main advantages is that it accommodates prior knowledge (in the form of Bayesian belief networks, prior probabilities for candidate hypotheses, or a probability distribution over observed data for a possible hypothesis). The classification of an unseen case is obtained through combined predictions of multiple hypotheses. It also scales up well with large data. It is an eager and supervised learning method and does not require search during learning process. Though it has no problem with noisy data, Bayesian learning has difficulty with small data sets. Bayesian learning adopts a bias that is based on the minimum description length principle.

3.6. Genetic Algorithms and Genetic Programming

Genetic algorithms and genetic programming are both biologically inspired learning methods. A target function is represented as bit strings in genetic algorithms, or as programs in genetic programming. The search process starts with a population of initial hypotheses. Through the crossover and mutation operations, members of current population give rise to the next generation of population. During each step of the iteration, hypotheses in the current population are evaluated with regard to a given measure of fitness, with the fittest hypotheses being selected as members of the next generation. The search process terminates when some hypothesis has a fitness value above some threshold. Thus, the learning process is essentially embodied in the generate-and-test beam search. The bias is fitness-driven. There are generational and steady-state algorithms.

3.7. Instance-Based Learning

Instance-based learning is a typical lazy learning approach in the sense that generalizing beyond the training data is deferred until an unseen case needs to be classified. In addition, a target function is not explicitly defined; instead, the learner returns a target function value when classifying a given unseen case. The target function value is generated based on a subset of the training data that is considered to be local to the unseen example, rather than the entire training data. This amounts to approximating a different target function for a distinct unseen example. This is a significant departure from the eager learning methods where a single target function is obtained as a result of the learner generalizing from the entire training data. The search process is based on statistical reasoning, and consists in identifying training data that are close to the given unseen case and producing the target function value based on its neighbors. Popular algorithms include: K-nearest neighbors, case-based reasoning, and locally weighted regression.

3.8. Inductive Logic Programming

Because a target function in inductive logic programming is defined by a set of (propositional or first-order) rules, it is highly amenable to human readability and interpretability. it lends itself to incorporation of background knowledge during learning process, and is an eager and supervised learning. The bias sanctioned by ILP includes rule accuracy, FOIL-gain, or preference of shorter clauses. There are a number of algorithms: SCA, FOIL, PROGOL, and inverted resolution.

3.9. Analytical Learning

Analytical learning allows a target function to be generalized from a domain theory (prior knowledge about the problem domain). The learned function has a good readability and interpretability. In analytical learning, search is performed in the form of deductive reasoning. The search bias in explanation-based learning, a major analytical learning method, is a domain theory and preference of a small set of Horn clauses. One important perspective of explanation-based learning is that learning can be construed as recompiling or reformulating the knowledge in the domain theory so as to make it operationally more efficient when classifying unseen cases. EBL algorithms include Prolog-EBG.

3.10. Inductive and Analytical Learning

Both inductive learning and analytical learning have their pros and cons. The former requires plentiful data (thus vulnerable to data quality and quantity problems), whereas the latter relies on a domain theory (hence susceptible to domain theory quality and quantity problems). Inductive analytical learning is meant to provide a framework where benefits from both approaches can be strengthened and impact of drawbacks minimized. It usually encompasses an inductive learning component and an analytical learning component. It requires both a training set and a domain theory, and can be an eager and supervised learning. The issues of target function representation, search, and bias are largely determined by the underlying learning components involved.

3.11. Reinforcement Learning

Reinforcement learning is the most general form of learning. It tackles the issue of how to learn a sequence of actions called a control strategy from indirect and delayed reward information (reinforcement). It is an eager and unsupervised learning. Its search is carried out through training episodes. Two main approaches exist for reinforcement learning: model-based and model-free approaches. The best-known model-free algorithm is Q-learning. In Q-learning, actions with maximum Q value are preferred.

3.12. Ensemble Learning

In ensemble learning, a target function is essentially the result of combining, through weighted or unweighted voting, a set of component or base-level functions called an ensemble. An ensemble can have a better predictive accuracy than its component function if (1) individual functions disagree with each other, (2) individual functions have a predictive accuracy that is slightly better than random classification (e.g., error rates below 0.5 for binary classification), and (3) individual functions' errors are at least somewhat uncorrelated. ensemble learning can be seen as a learning strategy that addresses inadequacies in training data (insufficient information in training data to help select a single best $h \in H$), in search algorithm (deployment of multiple hypotheses amounts to compensating for less than perfect search algorithms), and in the representation of H (weighted combination of individual functions makes it possible to represent a true function $f \notin H$). Ultimately, an ensemble is less likely to misclassify than just a single component function.

Two main issues exist in ensemble learning: ensemble construction, and classification combination. There are bagging, cross-validation, and boosting methods for constructing ensembles, and weighted vote and unweighted vote for combining classifications. The AdaBoost algorithm is one of the best methods for constructing ensembles of decision trees.

There are two approaches to ensemble construction. One is to combine component functions that are homogeneous (derived using the same learning algorithm and being defined in the same representation formalism, e.g., an ensemble of functions derived by decision tree method) and weak (slightly better than random guessing). Another approach is to combine component functions that are heterogeneous (derived by different learning algorithms and being represented in different formalism, e.g., an ensemble of functions derived by decision trees, instance-based learning, Bayesian learning, and neural networks) and strong (each of the component function performs relatively well in its own right).

3.13. Multiple Instance Learning

Multiple instance learning deals with the situation in which each training example may have several variant instances. If we use a bag to indicate the set of all variant instances for a training example, then for a Boolean class the label for the bag is positive if there is at least one variant instance in the bag that has a positive label. A bag has a negative label if all variant instances in the bag have a negative label. The learning algorithm is to approximate a target function that can classify every variant instance of an unseen negative example as negative, and at least one variant instance of an unseen positive example as positive.

3.14. Unsupervised Learning

In unsupervised learning, a learner is to analyze a set of objects that do not have their class labels, and discern the categories to which objects belong. Given a set of objects as input, there are two groups of approaches in unsupervised learning: density estimation methods that can be used in creating statistical models to capture or explain underlying patterns or interesting structures behind the input, and feature extraction methods that can be used to glean statistical features (regularities or irregularities) directly from the input. Unlike supervised learning, there is no direct measure of success for unsupervised learning. In general, it is difficult to establish the validity of inferences from the output unsupervised learning algorithms produce. Most frequently utilized methods under unsupervised learning include association rules, cluster analysis, self-organizing maps, and principal component analysis.

3.15. Semi-Supervised Learning

Semi-supervised learning relies on a collection labeled and unlabeled examples. The learning starts with using the labeled examples to obtain an initial target function, which is then used to classify the unlabeled examples, thus generating additional labeled examples. The learning process will be iterated on the augmented training set. Some semi-supervised learning methods include: expectation-maximization with generative mixture models, self-training, co-training, transductive support vector machines, and graph-based methods.

When a learner has some level of control over which part of the input domain it relies on in generating a target function, this is referred to as active learning. The control the learner possesses over the input example selection is called selective sampling. Active learning can be adopted in the following setting in semi-supervised learning: the learner identifies the most informative unlabeled examples and asks the user to label them. This combination of active learning and semi-supervised learning results in what is referred to as the multiview learning.

3.16. Support Vector Machines

Instead of learning a nonlinear target function from data in the input space directly, support vector machines uses a kernel function (defined in the form of inner product of training data) to transform the training data from the input space into a high-dimensional feature space F first, and then learns the optimal linear separator (a hyperplane) in F. A decision function, defined based on the linear separator, can be used to classify unseen cases. Kernel functions play a pivotal role in support vector machines. A kernel function relies only on a subset of the training data called support vectors.

Chapter 4

Intrusion Detection System

4.1. Background

Security concerns are becoming increasingly important in modern computer systems. With the development of networking and interoperation on public networks, security threats grow quickly. Fig. 1.1 shows the statistics of reported vulnerabilities [1] by Computer Emergency Response Team (CERT) at Carnegie Mellon University. In 2006, the number of reported vulnerability was 8,064 and in average, vulnerability was reported almost every hour. Security threats come from different parts, mainly from the flaw or bug in hardware or software, and incorrect configurations or operations of the system. On other hand, a series of security mechanisms were developed to defense security threats in different layers.

4.1.1. *Security defense in depth*

The term "intrusion" refers to attempts to compromise the confidentiality, integrity, availability of a resource, or to bypass the security mechanisms of a computer or network. Confidentiality is ensuring that information is accessible only to those authorized individuals, processes, or devices to have access. Disclosure to unauthorized entities, for example, using unauthorized network sniffing is a confidentiality violation. Cryptography is a kind of prevention technique to store and transmit confidential data. Integrity is having assurance that data has not been altered in transmission. Data integrity can be compromised when information has been corrupted, willfully or accidentally, before it is read by its intended recipient.

Digital signatures can be used to provide data integrity. Availability is assurance in the timely and reliable access to data services for authorized users. Denial of Service (DOS) is the typical attack aimed to resource availability.

Intrusion prevention techniques, such as user authorization/authentication (e.g., using password or biometrics), avoiding design/programming errors (e.g., clean room design), information protection (e.g., encryption), and firewall of network connection, were developed and used to protect computer system. However, intrusion prevention alone is not sufficient because as system becomes more complex, there are always exploitable weaknesses in the systems due to design and programming errors, wrong system configurations, or various "socially engineered" penetration techniques. The policies that balance convenience versus strict control of a system and information access also make it impossible for an operational system to be completely secure.

Intrusion detection tries to detect attempts to penetrate into a system, rather than prevent them from occurring by monitoring the events occurring in a computer system or network and analyzing them for signs of intrusions. It can generate and report alarms to system operators or security officers when it detects intrusion or abnormal activities. Some actions could be issued to block the ongoing attacks and/or minimize the damages of system. Unfortunately, the detection techniques are not perfect and some attacks still get through undetected.

After detecting an intrusion, disconnecting the computer from the network is the most effective way to block the intruder to compromise the system further. However, for some critical servers, it is impractical to disconnect it for every intrusion. The survivability of core services is under studying. Intrusion tolerant system is such a system, which tries to provide continued core services to critical users while under attack with a goal of some degradation of productivity.

Detect intrusion on a complex computer system is a hard problem. It is more difficult to discover what has been done exactly by an intruder on the computer system. Reinstall a fresh operation system is a good choice to get the security confidence of the computer system. However, it is a time consuming procedure to reinstall an operation system and recover all data. Some researcher works on the recoverability of component of system. The goal is to recover the damaged component of system without affecting other components.

4.1.2. *A brief history of intrusion detection*

The history of intrusion detection can go back to 1980s. In 1980, James Anderson first proposed to monitor security threats through audit trails [2]. In 1987, Dorothy Denning presented a general model [43] of an intrusion detection system, which analyzed audit trails to create profiles of users based on their activities. In 1988, Robert T. Morris released first Internet worm which disabled about 6,000 Sun and VAX workstations. The same year three IDSs, Intrusion Detection Expert System (IDES) [19] by SRI, Haystack [44] by University of California Davis, and Multics Intrusion Detection and Alerting System (MIDAS) [45] by National Computer Security Center were created. In 1990, Network Security Monitor (NSM) [46] analyzed network traffic to detect suspicious behavior. In 1991, Network Anomaly Detection and Intrusion Reporter (NADIR) [47] and Distributed Intrusion Detection System (DIDS) [48] collected and aggregated the audit data from multiple hosts to detect coordinated attacks against a set of hosts. The scalability, maintainability, efficiency, and fault tolerance of IDS were brought to the IDS researchers as the monitored system expended. In 1994 autonomous agents were proposed to address these problems [49] by Mark Crosbie and Eugene Spafford in Purdue University. In 1996, the Graph Based Intrusion Detection System (GrIDS) [50] aggregated network activities of interests into activity graph to detect the large-scale automated or coordinated attacks. In 1998, Ross Anderson and Abida Khattak used informational retrieval techniques in intrusion detection in [51]. Wenke Lee and Salvatore Stolfo applied data mining techniques to automatically construct intrusion detection models [25]. In 1999, mobile agents-based intrusion detection system was proposed to exploit the benefit from agent's mobility [52]. In the same year, the open source intrusion detection system Snort (www.snort.org) 1.0 was released. In 2000, the intrusion detection system was extended to wireless ad hoc network [53]. A non-cooperative game approach [54] was proposed to detect the intrusion in wireless sensor network in 2004.

4.1.3. *Classification of intrusion detection system*

Usually, intrusion detection systems are classified based on two aspects: detection approach and data source. According to the detection approach, an intrusion detection system can be anomaly detection, misuse detection or specification-based detection system.

The anomaly detection is concerned with identifying events that appear to be anomalous with respect to normal behavior of an entity such as a user or a host computer. The profile of a user entity, for instance, may include information such as the mean duration of his telnet and FTP sessions, the amount of bytes transmitted in both directions, the time of day or the terminals he usually logs-in from, etc. The profile of a host computer may include the average CPU utilization, the average number of logged-in users, and so on. The IDS monitors the operation of a computer system, and constantly compares the profile stored in its database. In case it detects a "large" deviation from the normal behavior, it signals an alarm to the system security officer. The magnitude of a "large" deviation is defined as a threshold set by the IDS or the system security officer. Usually the stored profiles are constantly being updated in order to reflect changes in user or system behavior. Since this model works by searching for sessions that are not normal, it is called an anomaly detection model.

The misuse detection characterizes a number of known attacks (misuse) to compromise a system and usually describes them as patterns. The way a known attack is represented to the system is an important characteristic of its operation. The variations include various types of graphs, regular expressions, etc. The implementation of such IDS usually involves an expert system that performs the matching against the stored rule-base. An obvious difficulty in this architecture is the need for constant updating of the rule-base, as new attack methods become known. Since the model operates by searching for patterns known to represent security attacks, it is referred to as a misuse detection model.

The second classification is based on the source of audit data of IDS. The original intrusion detection systems used to examine the audit data on a single machine and derive their conclusions based solely on that information, such IDS is called host IDS. Consequently, they could not detect attacks that were orchestrated by many sources, or attacks that span multiple machines in a network. Furthermore, they rely heavily on the logs provided by the underlying operating system, which renders them architecture-dependent and more vulnerable to Denial of Service (DOS) attacks against the IDS, since an intruder may manage to delay the logging mechanism, or even turn it off altogether. An efficient solution is provided by the IDS that passively monitor the network for suspicious activity, the IDS becomes network IDS. Since they depend solely on the ubiquitous TCP/IP protocol suite, they are literally architecture-independent and they can monitor heterogeneous networks quite naturally.

4.1.4. *Standardization efforts*

Even though intrusion detection has over 20 years history, there is no fully mature open standard for intrusion detection at present. However, two workgroups are doing some work on standards for IDS. Intrusion Detection Working Group (IDWG) is a working group in the Internet Engineering Task Force. The purpose of the IDWG is to define data formats and exchange procedures for sharing information of interest to intrusion detection and response systems, and to management systems which may need to interact with them [55].

The Common Intrusion Detection Framework (CIDF) is an attempt by the US government's Defense Advanced Research Projects Agency (DARPA) to develop an IDS interchange format used by DARPA researchers [56]. CIDF is not intended as a standard that would influence the commercial marketplace; it is a research project.

4.1.5. *General model of intrusion detection system*

Modern IDSs are extremely diverse in the techniques they employ to gather and analyze data. However, most of them follow the general model proposed by Dorothy E. Denning in 1987 [43]. The model consists of six main components: Subjects, Objects, Audit record, Profiles, Anomaly records, and Activity rules. Subjects are initiators of activity on a target system, including normal users and intruders. Objects are resources managed by the system, such as files, commands, devices, etc. Audit records are those data generated by the target system in response to actions performed or attempted by subjects on objects, for instance, user login, command execution, file access, etc. Profiles are some structures that characterize the behavior of subjects with respect to objects in terms of statistical metrics and models of observed activity. Profiles can be generated by hand with expert knowledge or produced automatically by some machine learning tools from some audit trial. Anomaly records are alarms generated when abnormal behaviors are detected. Actions can be taken when some conditions are satisfied according to the activity rules. Example actions include updating profiles, detecting abnormal behaviors, relating anomalies to suspected intrusions, producing reports, and so on.

4.2. Available Audit Data

Intrusion detection is the process of monitoring the events occurring in a computer system or networks and analyzing them for signs of intrusions. The events are issued by users (legitimate users or intruders) through commands or network. Most of those events will have change part of the system and even leave some traces on the system. We will discuss the possible audit data for intrusion detection from the system features, the user activities, and network activities.

4.2.1. *System features*

When we discuss the computer security, in most case, the hardware of the computer system is taken for granted to be secured by physical protection. The first interesting system feature of a computer system is its file system, which contains all software and data files. Unexpected changes especially to sensitive or seldom-modified portions of the file system (e.g., the system files) can provide clues in discovering attacks. Changes could include modifying, creating, or deleting directories and files. Intruders often create, substitute, modify, and damage files on systems to which they have gained access. For example, they may install backdoor programs or tools used to gain privileged access on the system. They may replace system programs with substitutes that perform the same functions but exclude information that could reveal their illicit activities. They also often modify system log files to remove traces of their activities. Each file has some attributes including access permission, i-node (for UNIX/Linux system), share links, user id, group id, file size, modification timestamp, and access timestamp. Although unchanged attributes do not guarantee nothing occurs to the file, unexpected changes of such attributes do indicate that something is wrong.

Software stored on disk is unlikely to cause damage until it is run. The only way to make system damage is though running programs that execute system calls, which are the gateway to privileged kernel operations, such as computations, transactions with files, devices, and other processes, and communications with processes on other remote systems. Every program implicitly specifies a set of system call sequences that it can produce. These sequences are determined by the ordering of system calls in the set of the possible execution paths through the program text [57]. For any nontrivial program, the theoretical sets of complete system call sequences will be huge, because it depends on the many aspects of process behavior, such as the parameter values, timing information, and so on. However, the local (short range) ordering of system calls appears to be remarkably consistent because of the code of most program is static and the system calls occur at fixed place within the code [58]. Thus the order of system call can also be used to detect some intrusions.

Every program executing on a system is represented by one or more processes. Each process executes with specific privileges that govern what system resources, programs, and data files it can access, and what it is permitted to do with them. Unexpected or anomalous system performance may indicate that an intruder is using the system covertly for unauthorized purposes. They may be attempting to attack other systems within (or external to) the network or they may be running network sniffer. A process that exhibits unexpected behavior may indicate that an intrusion has occurred. Intruders may have disrupted the execution of a program or service, causing it to fail or to operate in a way other than the user or administrator intended. For example, if intruders successfully disrupt the execution of access-control processes running on a firewall system, they may access your organization's internal network in ways that would normally be blocked by the firewall. Processes have some attributes including start-up time, arguments, issued command filenames, associated user id, exit status, time duration, and resources (CPU, memory, disk, time, file handle) consumed.

4.2.2. *User activities*

User issues commands to use a computer system. Different users tend to use different command sets and/or different command orders depending on their needs of the system. Intruder's behavior is naturally different from the legitimate user's normal behavior. A given user is acting in an abnormal manner when the actions of that user can be classified as intrusive and should be alerted. A user profile that represents a user's typical behavior can be created from its activities within a specified period. Then the profile can be used to detect possible intrusion or abnormality. For example, if the intrusion detection system has a profile that a given user usually logins to the monitored system at 8:00 am from a certain terminal. Then a remote login at 3:00 am under that user's account indicates some abnormality.

There might be some users who have similar needs of a computer system, for example, the students for a particular class, however, even two users who do the same thing may not use the same application program due to different applications available with the same functionalities.

For example, they write report using different editors or search the Internet using different browsers. In addition, the frequency with which command is used varies from user to user. In [23], the set of commands used and their frequency were used to identify the user, since this information reflects the task performed and the choice of application programs. And neural networks were trained to predict the next command for the user. Gebski and Wong [59] also demonstrate that the structure of the commands used could be analyzed to generate a model to test new commands.

Possible user activities include login/logout information (terminal, time, successful, failed attempts), changes in user identity, authentication status (such as enabling privileges), failed attempts to access restricted information (such as password files), keystroke features, commands issued (commands history, order and frequency), and violations of user quotas. Those activities information could be constructed from the user commands and their execution results.

4.2.3. *Network activities*

At current internet era, most of the computer systems are part of a kind of network. Attacks against those networked computer system could come from the inside legitimate users (sometimes, these attacks are called misuse) or from the intruders outside of the network who have successfully bypassed the intrusion prevention mechanism such as firework. When an intruder attacks a remote computer through network, each attack instruction is sent by network packets, so the network activities provide good resource to be analyzed to detect possible intrusion. Moreover, intruders from outside usually do reconnaissance in advance such as probes/scans the target network/computer system through network to identify the system configuration, such as hosts, network topology, operating systems, patches, and available services. An intrusion detection system could alert such malicious probe/scans through analyzing those reconnaissance network activities to stop further attacks.

Network packets include a variety of characteristics that can be used to find some intrusion information. For example, source address/port, destination address/port, packet size, protocol, option/flag, and the content of packets. To communicate successfully, each network packet should obey a certain communication protocol. There is no good reason to violate the protocol specifications. The protocol violations are often a result of an intruder using a network scanner in an attempt to bypass the firewall and to identify the type of systems on the networks. However, not all implementations of the same protocol follow the protocol specification strictly. Some intruder could attack against a specific implementation of a protocol with the legitimate packets. Network Security Monitor (NSM) [46] was the first system to use network packets directly as the source of audit data.

In some cases, investigating a single network packet is not enough to discover sublet intrusions because such single packet is legal and could be used normally. For example, we could "ping" a host by sending a single packet to know whether the host is ready to server us. However, sending a ping packet to every host within a certain IP range is definitely a suspicious activity to identify the available hosts in a network. Another example is the half-open connections of TCP connection. If a host grants the TCP connection request to a remote side, then the host is in "half-open" state to wait for the ACK packet from the remote side to set the connection. In this example, the remote user only sends a single request packet to the host, and for every TCP connection, such a request packet is necessary. However, the host takes some memory to maintain such half-open connection, and most operation systems have a limitation on the number of half-open connections. A malicious remote user could send lots of single TCP connection request packet to the host to reach the limitation, which is typical Denial-of-Service (DOS) attack, since after the limitation is reached, the host will deny any further TCP connection request. All network communications can be intercepted and recorded after they have been processed by the network stack in a computer host before they are passed on to application. Statistics on network packets also give much useful information to detection abnormal activities. Typical statistics include network traffic load (in or out), traffic distribution over different sources, protocols, applications and time, error counts, number of success and failure of authentication, etc. In addition, application logs for the corresponding network activities are valuable to detect intrusion.

4.3. Preprocess Methods

There are massive mounts of audit data available for IDS. Of course, some of them are useful but others are useless. At the other hand, different types of data are in different formats. In order to improve the performance of IDS, it is necessary to preprocess all of the available audit data into a specific format and reduce the amount of data to be analyzed. This is especially important if real-time detection is desired. One denial of service attack against IDS is to inject a large quantity of spurious data into a monitor event stream in order to distract the IDS while an attack on a monitored host takes place. Data reduction can occur in several ways: data filtering, feature extraction, feature selection, feature construction, and data grouping or clustering.

Data that is not considered useful can be filtered, leaving only the potentially interesting data. Some systems use heuristic or ad hoc methods to do data filtering, which can be viewed as expert rules for filtering. Other systems filter data in a more adaptive or dynamic way, such as use a neural network to filter data. Data filtering has the advantage of decreasing storage requirements and reducing processing time. However, filtering may throw out useful data.

Feature extraction is a process that extracts a set of new features from the original features through some linear or nonlinear transformations. The goal of feature extraction is to find a way to represent the original data in a more concise manner without loss of certain main aspects. Many techniques can be used in transformations. However, some transformations can only be applied to certain types of data. For example, multilayer perceptrons can be used for labeled nonlinear data. Clustering algorithm such as k-means can be used for non-labeled data. Principal Component Analysis (PCA) [60] is a classic technique to extract new features from linear combinations of the original features by finding eigenvectors from the covariance matrix of the data, where the eigenvector with the highest eigenvalue is the principal component of the data set. A feature vector consists of the first few eigenvectors with highest eigenvalues can be used as reduced data features. PCA had been used to reduce the feature space on the training data to build an intrusion detection system [61, 62].

Features may contain false correlations, which hinder the process of detecting intrusions. Some features may be redundant since the information they implied is contained in other features. Extra features will increase computation time and impact the accuracy of IDS. Feature selection is a process that chooses a subset of features from the original available features. The goal of feature selection is to reduce the feature space according to certain criterion, but it may improve the predictive accuracy of classification algorithms. For example, Wenke Lee reported a contrastive experiment in [26]. They found that the lean classifier with reduced feature set size had improved performance than the fat classifier with a very large size of features.

Feature construction is a process that discovers missing/hidden information about the relationships between features and augments that increase the space of features by inferring or creating additional features. There are various approaches to feature construction. They can be categorized into four groups: data driven, hypothesis driven, knowledge based, and hybrid. For example, specialized data mining programs are applied to audit data to compute frequent patterns describing correlations among features and records in [27], and then those frequent patterns are analyzed to construction additional features [121].

Clustering is the process of grouping a collection of data into distinct segments or clusters based on a suitable notion of closeness or similarity among these data. This process is also a data abstraction process to find a more compact representation of the set of objects. The characteristics of the clusters instead of the actual data can be stored and used to reduce original data.

4.4. Detection Methods

Modern systems primarily employ two techniques to perform intrusion detection: misuse detection and anomaly detection. Misuse detection, characterizes a number of known attacks (misuse) to compromise a system and usually describes them as patterns. Misuse detection system monitors for the appearance of explicit patterns. Such a system usually uses an expert system to identify intrusions based on a predetermined knowledge base. Therefore, misuse-based IDS have higher accuracy, but it could not detect any new intrusion without a pattern for the intrusion. Anomaly detection is concerned with identifying events that appear to be anomalous with respect to normal system behavior. Anomaly detection can identify new and previously unseen attacks. However, it is difficult to determine the boundary between acceptable and anomalous behavior at some time, so it will have higher false-positive rates. An experienced intruder could train an intrusion detection system gradually to let it accept an intrusive behavior as normal. In this section, we introduce the main ideas of some popular detection methods.

4.4.1. *Statistical analysis*

Statistical analysis attempts to quantify the acceptable behaviors on their statistical properties, such as limits, mean, and variance, and apply varied statistical test to identify observed behaviors which deviate significantly from the acceptable behaviors as intrusions. For example, we can record each occurrence of interesting events, such as network connections, CPU usage, network traffic load, failed login attempts, and open files when the system is running on an attack-free environment over a long time and calculate their limitations over a specific period. When the system is running in an environment with possible attacks, the number of occurrence of these interesting events during the specified period will be compared with the calculated limitations. If it is greater than an upper limit, then an alert on the intrusion could be reported. Of course, the statistical algorithm could be complicated. Statistics (called Q statistic) on different types of individual measure which represents different aspects of the system behavior are calculated by univariate statistical technique in IDES [19]. Those individual measures were grouped into four categories: intensity measures (track the number of occurrence), distribution measures (distribution of activity types), categorical measures (activity outcomes are categories, such as the name of accessed files), and ordinal measures (activity outcomes are counts, such as CPU time). And statistics on individual measures in different categories were calculated by different formulae. Another statistic (called S statistic) will be derived from the historical distribution of Q statistic to indicate whether the Q value on the current and near past audit data is unlikely or not. Since intrusions often affect multiple measures of activities collectively (such as the intensity measures and distribution measures in IDES), multivariate statistical analysis methods (chi-square test [17] and Hotelling's T2 test [18]) were presented to detect intrusion from host audit trails by identifying the anomalies involving multiple variables.

These approaches are useful to detect some intrusions, such as guess password (failed logins), and denial of service. Some simple statistics may be easily implemented and has lighter burden on hosts; other statistics may require complex computation and large memory (for example, the calculations on the covariance matrix in Hotelling's T2 test). Moreover, it is difficult to determine the threshold of the deviation and the time interval. Both of the threshold and the interval depend on the security-relevance of the event being monitored, as well as the historical number of occurrences. Statistical analysis alone is a poor detector of intrusions, and is usually implemented as a subcomponent of a large intrusion detection system, such as IDES [19], MIDAS [45], and NADIR [47].

4.4.2. *Expert system*

Expert Systems try to provide expert subject-specific knowledge, diagnoses, and recommendations for given real-world problem. Intrusion detection is a problem to diagnose the intrusion in a computer system. Most of earlier IDS built expert system to detect intrusion, such as IDES [19], MIDAS [45], and DIDS [48]. In those systems, the knowledge about attacks, system vulnerabilities and security policy were coded into knowledge base as if-then implication rules. The expert system is fact-driven reasoning system. The expert system deduction procedure starts from verifying that certain fields in the audit record (facts) match the condition part of rules in the knowledge base, if facts match one rule, then the rule will be applied in a way that either the associated action will be executed (reach the conclusion) or a new rule will be checked. For example, the expert system in IDES contains some rules to detect attempts of programmed login attacks by keeping track of unsuccessful logins and alerts the user when several failed logins occurs without an intervening successful login [19].

ID systems with expert system have higher accuracy, but it is expensive to produce the rule base and update the rule base by hand, since large amount existences of the inter-dependencies between different rules in the rule base. It is difficult to detect some subtle variations of known attacks due to the limitation of the security experts, and cannot detect any new attack not being coded in the rule base. The deduction performance may not good, because all rules are evaluated for each audit record (fact) due to the difficulty to efficiently specify an order of rules to match the audit record (the fact).

4.4.3. *Model-based system*

The attacks and system vulnerabilities in expert system are coded in if-then rules and the rules could be evaluated on the audit record directly. Model-based IDS attempts to model intrusions at a higher level of abstraction than audit records. It builds scenario models to represent the characteristic behavior of the intrusion. Each scenario comprises a sequence of behaviors making up an attack. The knowledge base is organized into different intrusion scenarios. The model-based scheme presented in [20] consists of three important modules: an anticipator, a planner, and an interpreter. The anticipator uses the scenario models (the knowledge base with specifications of intrusion scenarios) and active models (a set of scenario models such that the activities represented in the scenario model have been performed) to predict what behaviors are expected to occur in the next step according to the scenario. The planner then uses the predicted behaviors to determine how these behaviors will show up. The interpreter then translates predicted behaviors into system-dependent searchable evidences in the audit trail. When evidences are found in audit trail, the scenario model will be added to the active model and increase a measure of intrusion. An evidential reasoning calculus is used to update the measure of the attacks in the active models. When more and more evidences for intrusion attempts are accumulated and the measure crosses threshold, it signals an intrusion attempt [20].

Intrusion scenarios improve the maintainability on the knowledge base and the detection performance than expert system since the system knows what needs to be searched to match at each step, the large amounts of noise present in audit data can be filtered. A model-based ID system also has some limitations, since not all intrusion patterns could be organized into intrusion scenarios easily and the scenarios models may be bypassed by some intrusions with slight variant of attacks specified in scenarios models.

4.4.4. *State transition-based analysis*

This approach uses the attribute–value pairs to characterize system states. System states can be changed by performing some actions. An intrusion is viewed as a sequence of actions that changes the value of attribute(s), which lead the system state from an initial secure state to a target compromised state through zero or more intermediate states. The state in [21] is a snapshot of all kinds of memory location in the system in general, however, only partial of these attributes are required for a particular intrusion. The intrusion scenarios are represented in graph by state transition diagram in [21], where states (from initial state to possible intermediate state to the final compromised state) are connected by arcs. Each arc has associated with key action (called signature action). Signature actions are actions such that no action could be removed from the state transition graph to reach the compromised state successfully. These signature actions and interesting system fields will be searched in the audit data to match the intermediate/compromised state to detect intrusions. Such a system provides greater flexibility in identifying variations of known intrusions. The state transition diagrams to represent intrusions are intuitive in graph mode while identifying the requirements and compromises precisely and all the key actions are listed to complete the intrusion successfully. Also it has the ability to detect cooperating attackers and attacks across user sessions. However, it requires complex computation for determining each state transition and the number of the intermediate state will be very large for the complex intrusion and/or system. Only known intrusions could be analyzed to construct the state transition graph, further not all compromises could be represented by the system attributes purely to form a final compromised state.

A similar approach was presented in [10], where attack scenario is represented by the Color Petri Automaton (CPA), which is a kind of Colored Petri Nets with some restrictions, e.g., no concurrency. With terms used in Colored Petri Nets [63], the "places" in the CPA represent the system states and the "transitions" represent the events. The "transitions" may have some "guards" to update the system variables. The "places" and "transitions" are connected by arcs to represent the system state is changed from one state to another state by certain event. The "token" in the "place" indicates the current system state. The CPA model is portable and flexible, and new CPA for new signature could be added easily. Again the complexity of matching in CPA could increase exponential with the increasing size of the CPA to represent complicate signature.

4.4.5. *Neural network-based system*

An artificial neural network [64] consists of a large number of highly interconnected processing nodes working in parallel to solve specific problems. The output from each node could be nonlinear function result on its inputs. The inputs could be the output of other nodes or the input data directly. The interconnections could be unidirectional where only the outputs of nodes in one layer are fed into nodes in another layer in feed-forward network. The connections between the nodes could form a directed cycle as in the recurrent neural network. The neural networks solve problems in a different computing paradigm. They learn by examples without any program instruction to specific how to solve problems. The learning could be supervised where the example should be labeled such like the BP (error backpropagation) network and it could also be unsupervised where no label for example is needed such like SOM (self-organizing map [39]).

Different neural networks have been developed for intrusion detection [22, 23]. Recurrent neural networks were used to learn and predict the next command based on a sequence of previous commands by a specific user [22]. Through a shifting window, the network receives the most recent m commands as its input and predicts the next command. The recurrent network is constantly observing the new trend and "forgets" old behavior over time. The order of commands can vary a lot. In many cases, it is enough to recognize that the distribution of commands over the entire login session, or even the entire day, differs from the usual. Feed-forward neural network were build to identify an individual user from the distribution of used commands [23]. The numbers of use times of 100 commands were collected to form the command distribution for each user. A three-layer feed-forward neural network was trained on the command distributions with actual user id. After training, each new command distribution was fed to the network to output a user id who has matched command distribution in the training data. If the user is not the actual user or there is not clear suggestion (the outputs from network nodes are distinguishable), then an anomaly would be reported.

Neural networks learn by examples. We do not need to figure out a particular algorithm to detect intrusion from the audit data. We only need to prepare the training examples to train a neural network. However, the training result and the performance of neural network greatly depend on quality of the training examples. The examples must be selected and prepared carefully. It is also a labor-consume and error-prone work to label all training example for supervised learning.

4.4.6. *Data mining-based system*

Date Mining is the procedure of applying specific algorithms (data mining techniques) for extracting relatively simple but interpretable pattern from data. Both misuse detection and anomaly detection need to build patterns first, either for known intrusions, or for normal behaviors of users or system. Data mining techniques essentially are pattern discovery algorithm. Therefore, data mining techniques provide an alternative way to build patterns automatically other than manually. Just like neural network, patterns are discovered from data. However, unlike neural network where the knowledge learned from the training data is stored in the weight of connections in the neural network, discovered patterns by the data mining technique should be understandable and interpretable into useful knowledge by human being.

Several data mining techniques have been widely used in intrusion detection, for example, classification and clustering [24], associated rules [25], and frequent episode rules [26]. The goal of classification is to build a classifier from the training data to classify new data record to one existing class. Classifiers might have different representations. Two common representations of classifier are if-then rules and decision trees. The If-then rules check record attributes in their if-parts and predict class labels in their then-parts. A decision tree is a flow-chart-like tree structure, in which each node denotes a test on an attribute value, each branch represents an outcome of the test, and each leaf indicates a class label. Clustering will not rely on the labels of the training records, i.e., the training records are not need to be labeled. Clustering methods group records based on their similarity, so that the records in the same group/cluster have high similarity, whereas the records in different groups/clusters have quite low similarity. Whereas classification rule induction focuses on acquiring a capacity to make prediction, association rule discovery focuses on providing insight into the user. Specifically, it focuses on detecting and characterizing unexpected interrelationships between data elements. Classification rule induction typically uses heuristic search to find a small number of rules that jointly cover the majority of the training data. Association rule discovery typically used complete search to find large numbers of rules with no regard for covering training data. An association rule usually has the form: $X => Y$ [support, confidence], where X and Y are subset of attributes. The rule states that if a record satisfies X for those attributes included in X, then the record's attribute values included in Y should satisfy Y too. The support of the rule indicates the percentage of records that satisfy both left-hand side (X) and right-hand side (Y) of the rule over the all records in the training data set. The confidence of the rule indicates the percentage of the records that satisfy both left-hand side (X) and right-hand side (Y) of the rule over the all records that satisfy the left-hand side (X) in the training data set. While associate rule tries to represent the relation among the attribute of a record, the frequent episodes try to represent the relation on the inter-record for sequential data records. Again, like neural network, data mining-based system relies on the availability and quality of training data. The quality of discovered patterns is another issue. For example, associated rules will generate many trivial rules that are useless.

4.5. Architecture for Network Intrusion Detection System

Network IDS is a critical distributed system. Not only need it adapt the dynamic network environment, but also the quick emerged new attacks, even some attack targeting to itself. Varied architectures of NIDS have been proposed and implemented to improve the maintainability, scalability, efficiency, and resistance.

Centralized network intrusion detection systems are characterized by distributed audit collection and centralized analysis. Most, if not all, of the audit data is collected on the individual systems and then reported to some centralized location where the intrusion detection analysis is performed. The intrusion detection components on the multiple host systems are responsible for collecting the system information and converting it into a homogeneous form to be passed to the central analyzer. Examples of centralized NIDS include Network State Transition Analysis Tool (NSTAT) [21], Network Anomaly Detection and Intrusion Reporter (NADIR) [47], and Distributed Intrusion Detection System (DIDS) [48]. This architecture has two problems. It has the central point of failure. The centralized analysis component is the single point of failure and single target of an attack. Another problem is that it increases network workload because of passing massive audit data. Such architecture limits the ability of NIDS to scale up to handle larger network.

A hierarchical NIDS has some intermediate components between the collection and analysis components to form a tree structure hierarchy. The intermediate components aggregate, abstract, and reduce the collected data and output the results to analysis. For this architecture, the entire system must be partitioned into different and smaller segments by some ways, such as geography, administrative control, and collections of similar software platforms or anticipated types of intrusions. Examples of hierarchical NIDS include Autonomous Agents for Intrusion Detection (AAFID) [49], Graph-Based Intrusion Detection System (GrIDS) [50], Event Monitoring Enabling Responses to Anomalous Live Disturbances (EMERALD) [65], and most of commercial IDS. Hierarchical structures result in efficient communications, whereby refined information filters upward in the hierarchy and control downward. This architecture is excellent for creating scalable distributed IDSs with central points of administration.

In contrast to a hierarchical architecture, a netted architecture permits information flow from any node to any another node. Therefore, netted structures tend to suffer from inefficiency in communications, because of the unconstrained communication flow. However, they compensate for communications inefficiency with flexibility in function. In such an NIDS, e.g., Cooperating Security Managers (CSM) [66], the collection, aggregation, and analysis components are combined into a single component that is residing on every monitored system.

Mobile agents are a particular type of software agent with mobility, which is the capability to move from one host to another. In a mobile agent-based NIDS [67], all of collection, aggregation, and analysis components are wrapped by mobile agents. None of these components has to be continuously resident on a physical machine. The processing code can be migrated to a destination to reduce the network traffic instead of passing massive audit data. Mobile agent-based NIDS require that hosts and network devices be installed with a mobile agent platform. Mobile agent platform will manage and execute the mobile agent. Mobile agent-based NIDS can take advantages of using mobile code and mobile agent computing paradigm. Most attractive advantages include overcoming network latency, reducing network load, adaptive dynamically, and having robust and fault-tolerant behavior. Mobile agent-based NIDS also have some disadvantages. The obvious disadvantage is the security problem of mobile agent platform and mobile agents. Another concern is the performance. Mobile agent-based NIDS may not perform fast enough to meet the real-time requirement for NIDSs.

Part A

Intrusion Detection for Wired Network

In this part, we introduce the related work to these two problems identified in Chap. 1, and then present our system, ADAT IDS.

Chapter 5

Techniques for Intrusion Detection

5.1. Available Alarm Management Solutions

5.1.1. *Alarm correlation*

Most of current IDSs have multiple detection components, which have different focus and analyze different audit data. Each component will report alarms independently based on its analysis results. The alarm correlation is based on the observation that relationship existing among alarms reflects the relationship among attacks. Therefore, alarm correlation is a task to find the relationship among the alarms and give supports on analyzing the attacks implied by the alarms.

A hierarchical alert correlation system was introduced in [28] and integrated to EMERALD. To cope with the different importance of different features of alerts, a probabilistic minimum match criterion on features was proposed, which make system function as a rule-based correlation system. The system has the capability to tolerate slightly imperfect matches. The hierarchy of the system is defined as correlation within sensor, between sensor, and between sensor and attack step [28]. M-Correlator is another alert correlation component in EMERALD, which adopted a strategy of topology analysis, alert prioritization, and common attribute-based alert aggregation. In this component, not only the alerts from IDSs, but also from other security devices such as firewall, authentication services, and antivirus software are correlated. Three contributors of alert outcome, relevance score, and security incident priority score are organized into rank tree to record the knowledge of the alert [29].

A method so-called "prerequisites of intrusion" was applied to correlate the alarms in [30]. This method is based on the observation that in series

61

of attacks, there are logical connections between the attacks (early stages preparing for the later ones), so do the corresponding alarms [30]. They tried to organize the alarms into alarm scenarios to reflect the attack scenarios.

Statistical causality analysis (GCT for Granger Causality Test) has been performed on the aggregated alerts to discover new relationships among attacks in [31]. The GCT is time series-based causal analysis, which analyze the correlation between time series variables and discovering the causal relationships. The authors argue that attack steps that do not have well-known patterns or obvious relationships may nonetheless have some statistical correlations in the alert data [31].

To make full use of the available information, a formal data model called M2D2 was proposed for IDS alert correlation in [32]. In this data model, four types of information, characteristics of monitored system, monitoring tools, vulnerabilities, and observed event are included. Based on the data model, chronicles recognition was applied to correlate the alert in [33]. A chronicle is a set of events, linked together by time constraints, whose occurrence may depend on the context. Recognition of chronicles is based on a formalism in which time is fundamental.

Frequent episode is a data mining technique, which is developed to find patterns in event sequences. Frequent episode was also tried to mine the actionable knowledge from historical alarms to support the analysis of alarms. However, the result was not good in their experiments [34]. Due to the difficulty in defining the similarity between categorical features in the clustering, conceptual clustering was used to group alarms, which is particular good at handling categorical attributes such as IP addresses, port numbers. A modification of classic attribute-oriented induction was used as conceptual clustering tools in [34].

5.1.2. *Alarm filter*

Different from the alarm correlation, alarm filter try to filter most of false alarms, and reduce the amount of the alarms to be analyzed by operators. Association rules were mined within alarm burst in [35] based on the idea that frequent alarms over extended periods are likely to be normal. These association rules are subsequently used to implement anomaly detection on the IDS alarm stream.

A concept, root cause, had been borrowed from network management community and was applied to analyze the alarms in IDS [36]. Root cause of an alarm is the reason for which it occurs. The motive is based on the observation that root causes are mostly configuration problems and do not disappear unless someone fix them. A technique called alarm clustering was proposed to identify the root cause by grouping similar alarms [36]. The algorithm formalizes the similarities of different types of features in alarms, including categorical attributes, time attributes, and string attributes. The identified root causes serve as the filter to reduce the future alarms.

5.1.3. *Event classification process*

Actually, reducing false alarms is one of the most important goal for every IDS and every detection model. We have particular interest in the technique presented in [37]. An event classification process was proposed to reduce false alarm. The authors identify two reasons for the large number of false alarm of anomaly detection system, which usually contains a collection of models and needs to aggregate the different model outputs into a single, final result. The first reason is the simplistic aggregation of model outputs and the second one is the lack of integration of additional information in decision process. Based on their finding, a Bayesian network-based event classification process was proposed to replace the simple, threshold-based decision process. Instead of using a two-layer naïve Bayesian network, whose classification capability is same as a threshold-based system, the Bayesian network also models the inter-model dependence and integrates additional data. Therefore, the network structure becomes a directed acyclic graph other than a two-layer tree. Experiments on system calls were performed and the efficiency was demonstrated [37].

5.2. Available Performance Maintenance Solutions

5.2.1. *Adaptive learning*

For data mining-based IDS, training procedure usually takes quite long time, especially when the training dataset is quite large. However, when some new data is available, it is very desirable to be able to integrate the new information and make the existing IDS work better. Adaptive learning is a generic mechanism for adding new information to an existing system without retaining.

A "plug-in" method was proposed in [27]. When new intrusion emerges, a simple special purpose classifier is generated to detect only the new attack. The classifier is plugged or attached to the existing IDS to enable detection of the new attack. The main existing detection models remain unchanged. The new classifier participates the analysis of new data. The final prediction is a function of the predictions of both the old classifier and the new one. When a better model or a single model that can detect the new intrusion as well as the old intrusions is available later, the temporal model can be replaced or removed. This method is independent of the actual model-building algorithm. Different configurations have been experimented to test the effectiveness of this approach. The cost of training a simple classifier for one new attack was reported to be less than 150 times than training a monolithic classifier from all available data, and the accuracy of both is essentially equivalent [27].

5.2.2. *Incremental mining*

An anomaly detection component has the model of normal system or user behavior. As we have pointed out, the normal behavior could be changed from time to time. If the model keeps the same, it will launch false alarms for the changed normal behaviors.

Incremental mining technique was employed to constantly mine on the real-time data and update the detection profile in an adaptive IDS in [38]. The profile for the activity during an overlapping slide window is incrementally mined and the similarity between the recent profile and the base profile is measured. If the similarity stays above a threshold level, the base profile is taken to be a correct reflection of the current activities. When the similarity goes down below the threshold, it could be caused by attack, or by the normal changed behavior. To distinguish these two cases, the rate of change in the similarity is measured. If the change is abrupt, it is interpreted as an intrusion. The base profile will not be updated. If the change is gradual, then it is treated as normal change, and the base profile will be updated. A general incremental updating technique FUP_2 (for Fast Update Algorithm) was employed to update the base profile [38].

Chapter 6

Adaptive Automatically Tuning Intrusion Detection System

6.1. Architecture

Figure 6.1 depicts the system block diagram of our adaptive Automatically Tuning Intrusion Detection System (ADAT IDS). We include the system operator to show the interaction between the user and the system. The detection model is learned from the training data set. The prediction engine analyzes and makes prediction on each input data record according to the detection model. The prediction results are logged while the most suspect predictions are selectively reported to the system operator through prediction postprocessor. The system operator investigates the system and verifies the prediction results. The false predictions are then fed back to the fuzzy controlled model tuner. The model tuner automatically tunes the detection model according to the feedback received from the system operator.

With these two fuzz control [41] components (fuzzy prediction filter and fuzzy tuning controller [90]), our system will adaptively control the amount of the alerts (predictions) to be verified by the system user and adaptively tune the detection model when false predictions are verified.

6.2. SOM-Based Labeling Tool

A supervised learning system requires labeled training data. When a detection model to be built for a particular network, in order to improve the quality of the model to be built by a supervised learning system, the

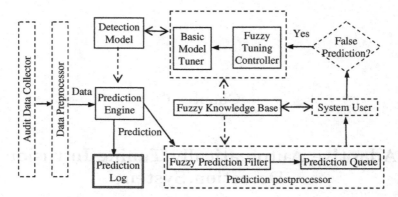

Fig. 6.1.   System block diagraph of our Adaptive Automatically Tuning IDS.

training data should be collected from that particular network and should be labeled before it is used to learn a model. We developed a labeling tool based on a clustering algorithm called Self-Organizing Map (SOM) to automatically label most of data from few of manually labeled data to reduce the effort required to verify all training data manually, while achieving low mislabeling rate.

Self-Organizing Map (SOM) essentially is a single layer feed forward artificial neural network, which was proposed by Teuvo Kohonen in 1982 [39]. It constructs a topology preserving mapping by unsupervised learning from the high-dimensional space onto its neurons (nodes) in such a way that relative distances between data points are preserved. The nodes usually form a two-dimensional regular lattice where the location of a node carries semantic information and SOM can thus serve as a clustering tool.

6.2.1. *Training algorithm*

An SOM consists of an array of nodes [39]. Each node contains a vector of weights with the same dimensionality as the input data. Given a set of data, training an SOM is a procedure to adjust the weights of the nodes to be similar with the input data. For any input data, the best matching node is selected according to its similarity to all other nodes. Then the radius of the neighborhood of the best matching node is calculated, which will decrease as the training procedure proceeds. Only weights of neighboring nodes are adjusted to make them more similar to the input data. This procedure is done for every training data and repeated many times to archive a better SOM. The high-level training algorithm is given in Fig. 6.2.

Given a training data set T with t input data $T = (V_{T1}...V_{Tt})$. Train an SOM M with m nodes $M = (V_{M1}...V_{Mm})$, where V_{Ti}, V_{Mj} are vectors with same sizes for any $1 \leq i \leq t$, $1 \leq j \leq m$.

```
FOR (j= 1, j<= m, j++) V_Mj = InitVector( );   // initialize the weight vector in SOM
WHILE ( !MeetStopCriterion( ) )
{
   iIterationCount ++;
   FOR ( i=1;i<t;i++) TrainSOM(V_Ti);
}

FUNCTION TrainSOM(v)
{
    FOR ( j= 1; j<= m; j++ ) Similarity[j]=CalculateNodeSiminility(V_Mj,v);
    bmu = BestMatchingUnit(Similarity[]);
    r = NeighborhoodRadius(V_Mbmu, iIterationCount);
    α = CalculateLearningRate(iIterationCount);
    FOR ( j= 1; j<= m; j++ ){
            θ = Neighborhood(j, r, bmu);
          V_Mj = UpdateVector(α, θ, v, V_Mj);
    }
} //End FUNCTION
```

Fig. 6.2. High-level SOM training algorithm.

The size of the SOM (the number of the nodes) is the first variable to be determined to train an SOM. However, it depends on the purpose and the user's choice. The weight vectors in SOM are usually initialized to small random values. To reduce the training time, the two largest principal component eigenvectors of the training set could be used to initialize the weight vector. The stop criterion is usually application specified. Some possible criteria include the iteration number, the threshold of the learning rate, the threshold of the sum, or the average of distances between the best matching nodes and input data. The similarity between two vectors is usually measured in their Euclidean distance of the two vectors. The neighborhood radius and learning rate should be decreased as the iteration count grows. The neighborhood function usually is a Bubble or Gaussian function.

The updating of the vector is governed by the following equation:

$$V_{Mj} = V_{Mj} + \alpha \times \theta \times (v - V_{Mj}), \tag{6.1}$$

where V_{Mj} is the weight vector of a node, v is an input vector, α is the current learning rate, and θ is the neighborhood value.

6.2.2. *Pre-cluster by symbolic features*

Similarity in the SOM is measured usually by the Euclidean distance between the input data and the node weight vectors, which works only on numerical features. However, audit data for intrusion detection usually contain several symbolic features, for instance, the connection protocol type, the service type, the source and destination IP address, and so on. In KDDCup'99 ID data set [40], nine out of 41 features are symbolic. Six of the symbolic features (att_land, logged_in, root_shell, su_attempted, is_host_login, and is_guest_login) are binary encoded with "1" or "0". For binary symbolic features, the distances on the encoded value are also binary, "0" indicates the same feature values and "1" indicates the different feature values. So the Euclidean distance still could be used to measure the similarity on these binary symbolic features. However, the other three symbolic features, feature "protocol type" has three different values, feature "service" has 66 different values and feature "flag" has 11 different values. Although we can encode these values into different numbers, for example, map protocol type "tcp", "udp", and "icmp" into 1, 2, and 3, respectively. The distances on these encoded values are no longer binary, and there are three distance values, "0", "1", and "2". "0" indicates same feature values. "2" indicates the greater difference than "1" does. Obviously, we cannot say that one protocol type (say "tcp") is more similar to another one (say "udp") than the third one (say "icmp"). Thus, the Euclidean distance is not suitable to measure the similarity on these features. It is these multiple values' symbolic features that require a preclustering step in our labeling tool to eliminate these features in the further clustering step by SOM. We adopt a perfect match policy on these symbolic features to precluster all data by the dot product on all these symbolic features. Only data with identical values on all these symbolic features will be grouped in the same preclustered set.

6.2.3. *Cluster by SOM*

After preclustering step in our label tool, the next step is to build SOMs to cluster data in preclustered sets. However, the first thing is to know whether SOMs should be built for some particular preclustered sets because the sizes of preclustered sets are quite different. There are 43 sets with one data record. Obviously, it is not needed to build SOMs for those sets. An SOM can only be used to cluster data in one set. But it cannot label a data record. Some manual efforts are required for each cluster to label them. In the other hand, clustering might make some errors because two data records might belong to different labels although they are in the same cluster. Thus for those preclustered sets with few data records, it cannot save much manual labor by clustering those data first. All data in those preclustered sets with few data records will be asked to label manually.

The size of each SOM (in terms of the number of nodes) should be chosen before SOMs can be constructed to cluster preclustered sets. The training algorithm can accept any given value as the size of an SOM, however, the size of an SOM has great impaction on the training time and the quality of the clusters. A small SOM takes less time than a big SOM to finish training on the same data set. However, in general, the clustering quality by the small SOM will be worse than the clustering quality by the big SOM. So the sizes of SOMs should depend on the amounts of data in preclustered sets. In our label tool, the initial size of an SOM is around 10% of the amount of data records in a set and the training stop criterion is the iteration number.

At the beginning, we implemented the SOM training algorithm as shown in Fig. 6.2. We observed that the data in many preclustered set are clustered into only a part of SOM nodes, while some distances between the datum and its clustering node were relatively very large. To eliminate those data with large distance in a cluster and make use of more nodes in an SOM, we modified the original SOM training algorithm to the one shown in Fig. 6.3. In this revised algorithm, after a training iteration, the updated SOM is used to cluster all data (ClusterDataset). Then the

```
FOR (j= 1, j<= m, j++) V_Mj = InitVector();   // initialize the weight vector in SOM
WHILE ( !MeetStopCriterion() )
{
    iIterationCount ++;
    FOR ( i=1; i<t; i++) TrainSOM(V_Ti); //train SOM by all input data in T
    ClusteringDataset(T);
    v = FindMaximalDistanceInput();
    n = FindMinimalNeighborEmptyNode();
    V_Mn = v;
    TrainSOM(V_Mn)
}
```

Fig. 6.3.   SOM training algorithm in our label tool.

input datum that has the maximal distance to its best matching node is selected (FindMaximalDistanceInput), and the node that has the minimal neighbor among the empty nodes such that no datum is clustered is found (FindMinimalNeighborEmptyNode). The weight vector of the selected empty node is set the same as the selected input. The SOM will be trained with the selected input (TrainSOM(VMn)).

After training an SOM, we need to evaluate the clustering quality to determine whether a new SOM should be trained. To build a new SOM, we can increase its size or/and iteration number, or just use different initial random weights. However, it usually will take more time to train a bigger SOM than train a small SOM on the same data set. Moreover, the more nodes usually form the more clusters, which require more human efforts to verify and label cluster seeds. In our label tool, when a new SOM is required, a new SOM will be trained with different initial weights first, if the clustering quality is still not satisfying, then the iteration number will be increased to train another new SOM, if the clustering quality is still not satisfying, a bigger SOM (more nodes) is the last choice. This procedure is not completely automatic, because a bigger SOM is to be trained by the user's request only. To help the system and the user to evaluate the clustering quality on data set by a trained SOM, the distance between every input data and its best matching node is calculated. Based on this individual distance, the minimal, average, and maximal distance to an input data and the distances' distribution are calculated for every best matching node and the data set. The system can train a new SOM with different initial weights and large iteration number based on the average distance. The user can check the distance distribution before request training a bigger SOM. Distance distribution is the count on the input data whose rate of the distance over the average distance is in some certain range.

6.2.4. *Label data in clusters*

Once we obtain a final SOM, every input datum is clustered around its best matching node with certain distance. However, the SOM can't infer the label of each cluster. The last step in our label tool is to label every input datum. In our label tool, data with different best matching nodes will not be merged to a larger cluster, i.e., data with same best matching node form a cluster. The cluster seed is the input data record which has the minimal distance to its node (the weight vector). The cluster seed must be verified and labeled manually. We assume that when input data record is verified manually, the label is correct. This label is then assigned to all other input data in the same cluster. In order to reduce errors, some selected input data are asked to be verified and labeled manually. The applied condition in our label tool is that the distance of an input is more than ten times of its lowest distance for the cluster, while the lowest distance for that cluster to its node is over twice the average distance in data set.

6.3. Hybrid Detection Model

Signature (misuse)-based intrusion detection uses signatures to model known attacks, while anomaly detection has models (profiles) for normal behavior of systems and/or users. Signature-based system is lack of the ability to detect new (unknown) attacks, while anomaly detection suffers volume of false alarms. We have developed a hybrid model (shown in Fig. 6.4) to detect intrusions from network connection data, which adopts a confidence-rated boosting-based binary learning algorithm, called SLIPPER (Simple Learner with Iterative Pruning to Produce Error Reduction) [82]. We use the available binary SLIPPER rule learning system to learn the binary classifier for normal network connection and intrusive connections [84, 85]. Multiple prediction confidence-based strategies were proposed and applied to arbitrate the final prediction among binary predictions from all binary classifiers.

6.3.1. *Binary SLIPPER rule learning system*

SLIPPER [82] is a rule learner that instantiated AdaBoost algorithm in [83]. Boosting algorithms try to improve the accuracy of any given

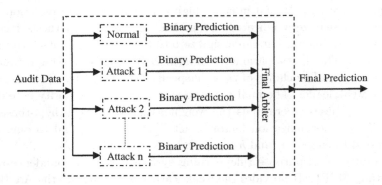

Fig. 6.4. Block diagram of our hybrid detection model.

Given: training set: $(x_1, y_1),...,(x_m, y_m)$; $x_i \in \chi$, $y_i \in \{-1,+1\}$

Initialize $D_1(i) = 1/m$.

For t = 1, ... , T

　　Train weak learner using distribution D_t.

　　Get weak hypothesis h_t: $\chi \rightarrow \Re$

　　　Choose $\alpha_t \in \Re$

　　　Update: $D_{t+1}(i) = D_t(i)\exp(-\alpha_t y_i h_t(x_i))/Z_t$; where Z_t is a normalization factor to make D_{t+1} be a distribution.

Output final hypothesis: $H(x) = sign(\sum_{t=1}^{T} \alpha_t h_t(x))$

Fig. 6.5.　　A generalized version of AdaBoost.

learning algorithm using the ensemble of a set of weak prediction rules other than one single highly accurate rule, because it is much easier to find a roughly true rule other than to find one single highly accurate rule. All weak prediction rules are learned by running the given learning algorithm repeatedly on different distributions over the training data. The earlier boosting algorithms were developed for theoretical reasons. While mathematically beautiful, these algorithms were rather impractical.

The AdaBoost algorithm (shown in Fig. 6.5) was proved as a practically useful algorithm.

The label of data (y) in the training set is binary, represented by -1 or $+1$. The $h_t(x)$ in Fig. 6.5 could be a real value rather than binary. In binary classification problem, the sign of $h_t(x)$ is interpreted as the predicted label while the magnitude $|h_t(x)|$ gives a measure of confidence for the prediction. Large numbers for $|h_t(x)|$ indicate high confidence in the prediction, and numbers close to zero indicate low confidence. If a weak hypothesis does not fire on a data instance, it can assign zero to $h_t(x)$ to abstain itself from the prediction. The α_t is a parameter to intuitively measure the importance of hypothesis h_t. The choice of α_t is unspecified deliberately, which depends on the weak leaner. The final hypothesis is a weighted majority vote of all weak hypotheses where α_t is the weight assigned to weak hypothesis h_t. The Z_t is a normalization factor to let $\sum D_{t+1}(i)$ be equal to one. It is suggested to choose α_t and h_t on each boost to minimize Z_t.

As a general-purpose rule-learning system based on confidence-rated boosting, SLIPPER provides the weak learner to instantiate the AdaBoost algorithm. The weak learner is essentially the same process as used in the inner loops of IREP and RIPPER [72]. It splits the training data randomly into two disjoint subsets. One subset is used to build a single rule to cover no negative example or no further refinement. The rule is pruned in the other subset immediately. Unlike some other conventional rule learners, the covered examples are not removed from the training set. They are given lower weights in the further boosting. The quality metric for rules encompasses a natural trade-off between accuracy and coverage. A rule will abstain on examples that are not covered by the rule, thus the label assigned to an instance depends only on the confidence of the rules that cover that instance. Only positive class predictions will be made by the learned rule set, while a single default rule is used to predict negative class examples.

The hypotheses are rules, which make the models understandable. In SLIPPER, a rule R is forced to abstain on all examples unsatisfied by R through setting zero to $h_t(x)$, while to predict with the same confidence C_R on every example satisfied by R, i.e.,

$$C_R = \begin{cases} \alpha_t h_t(x) & \forall x \in R \\ 0 & \text{if } x \notin R \end{cases}. \tag{6.2}$$

To minimize training error, according to the suggestion, in SLIPPER, the goal is to find a single confidence value of CR to minimize Z_t instead of finding two values α_t and h_t. After omiting the dependency on t, Z is rewritten in SLIPPER as:

$$Z = W_0 + W_+ \exp(-C_R) + W_- \exp(+C_R), \tag{6.3}$$

where $C_R = \alpha h(x), W_0 = \sum_{x_i \notin R} D(i), W_+ = \sum_{x_i \in R:y_i=+1} D(i)$, and $W_- = \sum_{x_i \in R:y_i=-1} D(i)$.
To minimize Z, the C_R should be set by:

$$C_R = \frac{1}{2} \ln \left(\frac{W_+}{W_-} \right). \tag{6.4}$$

In practice, $1/2n$ is added to both W_+ and W_- to prevent extreme confidence as following:

$$C_R = \frac{1}{2} \ln \left(\frac{W_+ + 1/2n}{W_- + 1/2n} \right), \tag{6.5}$$

where n is the total number of data records in the training set. In SLIPPER, only the rule with positive confidence C_R will be computed from the weak learner, else a default rule with negative confidence will be returned in the prune stage. The final hypothesis is:

$$H(X) = sign \left(\sum_{R_t : x \in R_t} C_{R_t} \right). \tag{6.6}$$

In prediction step, the sign of $H(X)$ is interpreted as the predicted label on data X, while the magnitude $|H(X)|$ is the prediction confidence (PC). When the sign is a plus $(+)$, we refer this prediction as positive prediction. A negative prediction means the sign is a minus $(-)$.

6.3.2. *Binary classifiers*

A binary version of SLIPPER rule learning system for academic and research use is available for download on webpage http://www.cs.cmu.edu/~wcohen/slipper. The binary SLIPPER rule learning system can learn binary classifier from labeled training data. For intrusion detection, the primary task is to detect intrusive one from normal activities, however, not all of successful intrusions damage the system at the same severe level. Usually intrusions are categorized into DOS, PROBE, U2R, and R2L. It is desired that the IDS will report alarms on intrusions with proper type. System security officers pay different attentions on different types of alarms of intrusions. For example, most of security officers will just collect "Probe" alarms but do nothing else on these alarms. However, they will investigate the system when an "r2l" alarm is reported to make sure whether it is a false alarm and execute defense actions on true alarms. So intrusion detection is no longer a binary classification problem. Our hybrid detection model consists of multiple binary classifiers and a final arbiter. The binary classifiers were learned from training data set using the SLIPPER rule learning system. The final arbiter is to choose one of the results from those binary classifiers as the final result. The building process of binary classifiers on KDDCup'99 data set will be introduced in the next section. We will discuss our proposed final arbiters in this section.

As we discussed above, in prediction step, a binary classifier will output the predicted label and the prediction confidence in a single signed real value (From this point, we refer this signed real value as prediction confidence.).

6.3.3. *Final arbiter*

Before discussing any arbitral strategy, let us take a look how many different cases we need to deal with. A binary classifier will output only two results.

For a detection model with n binary classifiers, there are total 2^n different prediction permutations. If each binary classifier has the same weight in choosing the final prediction, then the number of different cases drops to n. In formally, let k be the number of positive predictions (with positive prediction confidence) for one unseen example, then k can be varied from 0 to n. Further, we can categorize them to three different cases according to the value of k, namely, $k = 0$, $k = 1$, and $k > 1$. The first case ($k = 0$), none of the predicted classes is its corresponding positive class. The second case ($k = 1$), only one of the predicted classes is its corresponding positive class. The third case ($k > 1$), more than one predicted classes are its corresponding positive class.

6.3.3.1. *Arbitral strategy by prediction confidence*

The first case happens because the unseen example is much different from all of the training examples. However, the degree of difference for each classifier model might be different, i.e., the confidences of all predictions might not be the same. If the predicted class is not the positive class, the higher the confidence is, the higher probably the example does not belong to this class. Therefore, we can choose the predictions with lowest confidence as the final prediction in this case. Because the prediction confidence of binary model is negative when the predicted class is its negative class, we choose the prediction with the highest negative prediction confidence as the final class. The algorithm is shown in Fig. 6.6.

It is trivial to deal with the second case. We can directly choose the positive class as the final prediction, because the example is similar with examples in one of the subset of the training data, but different from other examples. When there is only one positive prediction, then this positive confidence must be greater than any other negative confidences. The algorithm in Fig. 6.6 works on this case.

Input: Prediction Confidences: PC_1, PC_2 ... PC_n and Class Set C
Output: Final Prediction Class Name

$$i = \{\, j \mid PC_j = MAX\ \{PC_1, PC_2 ..... PC_n\}\,\}$$

Return C_i.cname

Fig. 6.6. Final arbitral strategy by prediction confidence.

The third cases also will occur due to the coverage overlap of different models. Again, the degree of similarity in different binary models might not be the same. Therefore, the confidences of different predictions are different. In this case, we only need to consider those predictions with positive class. If the predicted class is the positive class, the higher the confidence is, the higher probably the example belongs to this class. Therefore, we can choose the prediction with highest confidence as the final prediction in this case just like the algorithm shown in Fig. 6.6.

With this final prediction strategy, our detection model should work on prediction step. Nevertheless, this strategy is not fair to all binary classifiers because we compare the prediction confidences from different binary classifiers. For predictions from one classifier, the SLIPPER rule learning system guarantees that the large magnitudes of the confidence value indicate high confidence in the prediction, and the numbers close to zero indicate low confidence. However, in our hybrid detection model, the prediction confidences come from different binary classifiers. Nevertheless, these binary classifiers are related in some degree. They are trained using the same algorithm on the intrinsically same data set. We can safely say that it is only roughly correct that larger magnitude of the confidence indicates the higher prediction confidence. Based on this consideration, we propose our second strategy based on prediction confidence ratio, which is a relative value.

6.3.3.2. *Arbitral strategy by prediction confidence ratio*

At the end of the last subsection, we point out that the prediction confidences from different classifiers are not strictly comparable. It will be clearer when we take a look how the prediction confidence generates. From the SLIPPER algorithm, we can see that the prediction confidence is the sum of the confidences of all rules that cover the unseen example. However, different classifiers have different rule sets. Rules in one rule set except the default rule are trained to cover examples in its training data set.

To take advantage of the prediction confidence to determine the final prediction, we introduce the ratio of the prediction confidence with the maximal confidence of its prediction from one classifier. The higher ratio from one classifier indicates the higher possibility for the unseen example to be that classifier. Now we need to find the maximal confidence for each classifier.

r2l	1775.6	0	IF	service = other	logged_in = 1
r2l	755.992	0	IF	service = imap4	count <= 4
r2l	283.005	0	IF	service = login	duration >= 67

Fig. 6.7. Rules with mutually exclusive conditions.

When the binary classifier is used to predict an example, the sum of the confidence of all rules that cover the example in the binary classifier is calculated, one way to get the maximal confidence of positive prediction is to sum up all confidences of all rules in the classifier and use the confidence of the default rule as the maximal confidence of non-positive prediction. But probably there are some rules in the same classifier that they cannot cover any same example because of their mutually exclusive conditions, as examples listed in Fig. 6.7, which are excerpt from a binary classifier learned from KDDCup'99 ID data set. Therefore, this kind of maximal confidence might not be reached in practice.

To find a reachable maximal confidence, we turn to the training data set. After each binary classifier is trained, the classifier is applied on its training data set to get the maximal prediction confidences of positive prediction and non-positive prediction. Then use these maximal confidences to compute the prediction confidence ratio (PCR) by Eq. (6.7):

$$PCR_j = PC_j/MAX\{PC_j^1, PC_j^2, \ldots, PC_j^m\}. \tag{6.7}$$

PC_j stands for prediction confidence of prediction engine j on the data record in test data set. While PC_j^m stands for the prediction confidence of prediction engine j on all data from m-th example in the training data set. After getting the confidence ratio, we can choose the final prediction according to the prediction confidence ratio. The algorithm is same as shown in Fig. 6.6, but the inputs are confidence ratios instead of prediction confidence. We choose the positive prediction of the classifier whose confidence ratio is the highest for each unseen example. If all of the confidence ratios are negative, we choose the positive class of the classifier whose magnitude of the confidence ratio is lowest. We believe that if an example has the lowest confidence not belonging to one class, it is more probably that this example belongs to this class than to other classes. Formally, this final arbitral strategy can be expressed as follows:

$$i = \{j|PCR_j = MAX\{PCR_1, PCR_2, \ldots, PCR_n\}\}, \tag{6.8}$$

where PCR_j is prediction confidence ratio and computed by Eq. (6.7), and i is the index of the binary classifier whose prediction result is selected to be the final prediction result. We propose these two prediction strategies because we treat the problem as a linear separable one. The algorithm is simple and the computation workload is light. However, we cannot prove that this problem is strictly linear separable problem from the SLIPPER algorithm. Based on this consideration, we proposed our third final prediction strategy (BP network) and discussed it in the next subsection.

6.3.3.3. *Arbitral strategy by neural network*

Artificial Neural network is a powerful tool to solve complex classification problem. We do not need to force much assumption to the problem. We only need to prepare a set of inputs and targets to train it, and let the neural network learn a model from the training data to classify the inputs.

The most popular type of neural network is the error back-propagation (BP) neural network. A conventional BP network is a three-layer feed forward network. BP network works well for classification problem. We choose to build a conventional BP network as our final arbiter because of its simplicity and popularity. The inputs of the BP network are the prediction confidence ratios from each binary model. The maximal output is interpreted as the final prediction class.

The number of nodes for the input layer and the output layer is the number of binary models in our detection model. However, it is difficult to choose the best number of nodes for the hidden layer, because it depends on many facts, such as the numbers of nodes in input and output layers, the number of training examples, the type of hidden node activation function, and so on. Some researchers suggest some rules of thumb for choosing the number of nodes for hidden layer. For example, "the size of hidden layer to be somewhere between the input layer size and the output layer size"; and "the number of hidden nodes is the sum of input size and output size times $2/3$". The structure of our BP network is shown in Fig. 6.8.

The formal expression of the final arbitral strategy by BP network is shown below:

$$i = \{j|NNO_j = MAX\{NNO_1, NNO_2, \ldots, NNO_n\}\}, \qquad (6.9)$$

where $NNO_j = \Sigma_k(\omega_{jk} \cdot \Sigma(\omega_{kl} \cdot PCR_l))$ stands for the output of the neural network via the output node $j \cdot \omega_{jk}$ and ω_{kl} are weights on the

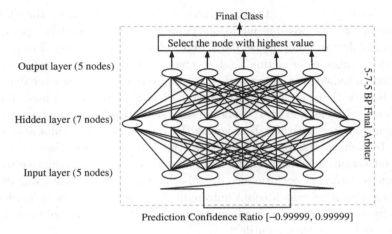

Fig. 6.8.   BP Networks structure.

connection between output node j and hidden node k and the connection between hidden node k and input node l, respectively. Suppose there L input nodes, K hidden nodes and J output nodes, then compared to the arbitral strategy by prediction confidence ratio, arbitral strategy by BP network costs $(L * K + K * J)$ more multiplications and additions on every example.

6.3.4. *Detection model tuning*

In the end of last chapter, we conclude that the detection model has to be tuned continuously to maintain the decent performance on detecting intrusion. For commercial products (mainly signature/misuse-based IDS), the main tuning method is to filter out signatures to avoid generating noise [86] and to add new signatures. In data mining-based intrusion detection, system parameters are adjusted to balance the detection rate and the false rate. Such tuning is coarse and the procedure must be performed manually by the system operator. Other methods, such as plugging in a special purpose sub-model [27] or superseding the current model by dynamically mined new models [38], are also introduced in section 5.2. Training a special purpose model forces the user to collect and construct high quality training data. Mining a new model in real-time from unverified data incurs the risk that the model could be trained by an experienced intruder to accept abnormal data.

The value of an intrusion detection system is to alert the system operator on any possible intrusion. However, it is the system operator's responsibility to analyze the alarm and judge its truthfulness. The system operator takes some action against true intrusion, such as stop ongoing intrusion, remedy the monitored computer system, and reduce the damage. We believe that the efforts of operator of IDS to verify the false alarms are also valuable, and an IDS should take advantage of the analysis results to improve itself, rather than ignore the quite valuable results and leave the burden to the operator to tune the IDS manually. Based on this consideration, it is desirable to make the detection model adaptive to the previous detection performance. In this chapter, we will discuss our model tuning algorithm which could automatically tune the detection model on the fly according to the feedback provided by the system operator when false predictions were identified.

6.3.4.1. *Observations*

The following properties of the performance of individual rules with respect to binary predictions were observed.

Property 1: Isolated false predictions exist for most rules and can amount to about 25% of all false predictions.

Property 2: Often, false predictions come in long successive prediction sequences. Long successive false prediction sequences provide an opportunity for our system to benefit from model tuning.

To analyze the performance of an individual rule on adjacent data, we logged the data coverage rate and the false rate of each rule on every 500 data records. The entire test data set was divided into 623 sequential segments of 500 data records. We analyze the test performance of each rule and observe yet another property.

Property 3: The false rate of a rule might change dramatically even in adjoining segments.

We will explain these three properties by an example. The test performance of rule 29 in binary classifier "BC-Normal" on a subset of the data is shown in Fig. 6.9. The left vertical coordinates showing data coverage uses logarithmic scale. The test data start from segment 230 and runs to segment 294. Rule 29 covers 71,205 out of 311,029 test data records (22.89%), which are distributed among 267 segments out of all 623 segments (42.86%). 17,343 out of 71,205 (24.36%) final predictions on the

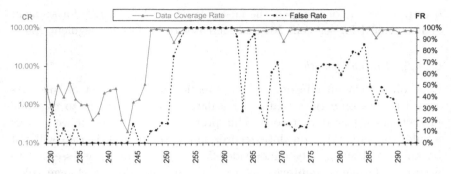

Fig. 6.9.   Performance of Rule 29 of "BC-Normal" on Binary Prediction.

corresponding data records covered by rule 29 are false predictions. Rule 29 covers 20,987 out of 32,500 (64.58%) test data records in the 65 segments shown in Fig. 6.8. A total of 11,750 out of 20,987 (55.98%) final predictions on the corresponding data records covered by rule 29 in these 65 segments are false predictions.

We first examine segments 230 through 232. The false rates on these three successive segments are 0%, 33%, and 0%, respectively. Only three data records are covered by rule 29 in segment 231. The false prediction in this segment is an isolated false prediction. Note that isolated false predictions exist in many segments, but cannot easily be shown in Fig. 6.9.

Property 2 states that the false predictions made on data records covered by most of rules are not distributed evenly on the entire test data set, instead, they come in clusters. For rule 29, 11,750 out of 17,343 (67.75%) false predictions are made on the data records in these 65 segments. The fact that 67.75% false predictions occur within 65 successive segments out of 267 (24.34%) segments also demonstrates Property 1 and is explicit in Fig. 2.4 by the extreme high false rate (99–100%) in the segments 254 through 262. Property 2 is helpful for model tuning to reduce false predictions. Using our tuning algorithm, the model is able to make true predictions on the data records in segment 254 after a few rounds of tuning rule 29. Once the updated model makes true predictions, the model will keep making true predictions on all subsequent data records until it makes a false prediction on a data record that the original model made a true prediction on.

Fig. 6.9 also exhibits Property 3. Although the overall false prediction rate is 55.98% in these 65 segments, the false rate on a segment varies from

0% up to 100%. For instance, the false rate drops from 92.12% for segment 263 to 27.60% for segment 264 and increases to 87.33% for segment 265.

6.3.4.2. *Tuning algorithm*

Each binary classifier in our hybrid detection model is a set of rules. As shown before, only rules that cover a data record contribute to the final prediction on this data record. This property ensures that if we change a rule, the prediction on data records not covered by this rule will not be affected. Having only minor side-effects during tuning is essential to ensure performance improvement from tuning. We do not change rules; new rules can be learned using other methods, such as incremental learning techniques, should such prove necessary. During tuning, we change the associated confidence values to adjust the contribution of each rule to the binary prediction. Consequentially, tuning ensures that if a data record is covered by a rule in the original model, then it will be covered by this rule also in the tuned model and vice versa. To limit possible side-effects, we only change the associated confidence values of positive rules as a default rule covers every data record.

In SLIPPER, each rule has two parameters, learned from the training data set, named W_+ and W_-, which represent the total weight of the positive and negative examples covered by the rule, respectively, when the rule was constructed. The confidence is "smoothed" to avoid extreme confidence value by adding a tiny value ε as:

$$C_R = \frac{1}{2}\ln\left(\frac{W_+ + \varepsilon}{W_- + \varepsilon}\right). \tag{6.10}$$

When a binary classifier is used to predict a new data record, two different types of false predictions may be generated according to the sum of confidence values of all rules that cover this data record. When the sum is positive, the binary classifier predicts the data record to be in the positive class. If this prediction is false, it is treated as a false-positive prediction and labeled as "P". When the sum is negative, the binary classifier predicts the data record to be in the negative class. If this prediction is false, it is considered as a false-negative prediction and labeled as "N". We use the label "T" to indicate a true prediction. The sequence of prediction results can then be written as: ... $\{P\}^l\{N\}^i\{T\}^j\ldots$, where $l > 0$, $i, j \geq 0$, and $i + j > 0$. Obviously, when the classifier makes a false-positive prediction, the confidence values of those positive rules involved should be decreased to avoid the false-positive prediction made by these rules on subsequent data. When the classifier makes a false-negative prediction, the confidence values of the positive rules involved should be increased to avoid false-negative predictions made by these rules on successive data. Formally,

$$C'_R = \begin{cases} p \cdot C_R & \text{if } R \propto \text{P} \\ q \cdot C_R & \text{if } R \propto \text{N} \end{cases}, \qquad (6.11)$$

where $p < 1, q > 1$ and $R \propto \text{P}$ implies that a positive rule R contributes to a false-positive prediction. We multiply a pair of relative values (p and q) with the original confidence values to ensure that new confidence values remain positive although they may be very small when the adjustment procedure is repeated many times in the same direction.

If the updating is performed n times, the sum of the confidence values of positive rules will be:

$$\sum C'_R = \begin{cases} p^n \cdot \sum C_R & \text{if } R \propto \text{P} \\ q^n \cdot \sum C_R & \text{if } R \propto \text{N} \end{cases}. \qquad (6.12)$$

Because $p < 1, q > 1$, and the confidence value of the default rule is unchanged, trivially there exists a number n, such that after updating the confidence values n times, the sign of the sum of the confidence values of all rules (both positive rules and the default rule) will be changed. That means the tuned classifier could make a true prediction on the data where the original classifier made a false prediction. Formally, $\exists n, (\{\text{P}\}^n)_o =>$ $(\{\text{P}\}^{n-1}\text{T})_t$, where $(\ )_o$ represents the sequence of prediction results based on the original classifier and $(\ )_t$ stands for the sequence of prediction results from the tuned classifier.

6.3.4.3. *An instance of tuning algorithm*

The number of choices for the pair of values p and q is large. For example, we might choose 0.75 and 1.5 to adjust confidence values conservatively or we might choose 0.25 and 4 which adjusts the confidence values more aggressively. Confidence values could also be adjusted by relying on dynamic relative values. In our experiments, we set $p = 0.5$ and $q = 2$. According to Eq. (6.11), p can be any value greater than 0 but less than 1. We choose the middle value for p to avoid aggressive updating yet keep tuning efficient. We set q to be $1/p$ to ensure that the original confidence value is restored when it turns out that tuning had led to an incorrect prediction and the rule is subsequently tuned again to yield the original prediction.

When a false-positive prediction is made on a data record, from the point of view of training this data is a negative data record for those rules that cover the data but misclassified it as a positive data record. Therefore, we can move some weights from W_+ to W_- while keeping the sum of weights unchanged as follows:

$$\begin{cases} C'_R = \dfrac{1}{2}\ln\left(\dfrac{W'_+ + \varepsilon}{W'_- + \varepsilon}\right) = p \times C_R = \dfrac{1}{2} \times \dfrac{1}{2}\ln\left(\dfrac{W_+ + \varepsilon}{W_- + \varepsilon}\right). \\ W'_+ + W'_- = W_+ + W_- \end{cases} \qquad (6.13)$$

Solving the above equations we can get the new W'_+ and W'_-,

$$\begin{cases} W'_+ = \dfrac{\sqrt{W_+ + \varepsilon}}{\sqrt{W_+ + \varepsilon} + \sqrt{W_- + \varepsilon}} \times (W_+ + \varepsilon + W_- + \varepsilon) - \varepsilon \\ W'_- = \dfrac{\sqrt{W_- + \varepsilon}}{\sqrt{W_+ + \varepsilon} + \sqrt{W_- + \varepsilon}} \times (W_+ + \varepsilon + W_- + \varepsilon) - \varepsilon \end{cases} \qquad (6.14)$$

Similarly, if a false-negative occurs, then each fired rule, except for the default rule, should double its associated confidence. Because this datum is a positive example for those fired rules but misclassified as a negative example in the training viewpoint, we can move some weights from W_- to W_+ while keeping the sum of weights unchanged as follows:

$$\begin{cases} C'_R = \dfrac{1}{2}\ln\left(\dfrac{W'_+ + \varepsilon}{W'_- + \varepsilon}\right) = q \times C_R = 2 \times \dfrac{1}{2}\ln\left(\dfrac{W_+ + \varepsilon}{W_- + \varepsilon}\right). \\ W'_+ + W'_- = W_+ + W_- \end{cases} \qquad (6.15)$$

Again, solve above equations we get the new W'_+ and W'_-,

$$\begin{cases} W'_+ = \dfrac{(W_+ + \varepsilon)^2}{(W_+ + \varepsilon)^2 + (W_- + \varepsilon)^2} \times (W_+ + \varepsilon + W_- + \varepsilon) - \varepsilon \\ W'_- = \dfrac{(W_- + \varepsilon)^2}{(W_+ + \varepsilon)^2 + (W_- + \varepsilon)^2} \times (W_+ + \varepsilon + W_- + \varepsilon) - \varepsilon \end{cases} \qquad (6.16)$$

6.3.4.4. *Performance estimation*

Because confidence values are updated after the user identifies a false prediction and the tuned classifier cannot be used to predict the data again when the original classifier made a false prediction, the benefit of such tuning depends on the subsequent data. Note that $(PN)_o => (PN)_t$ as the classifier decreases the confidence values after it makes a false positive prediction. (We only discuss the tuning after a false-positive prediction; tuning after a false-negative prediction is similar.) Assume that tuning is aggressive by setting appropriate values for p and q in Eq. (6.11). After tuning on a false-positive prediction, the classifier would make a true prediction on the data over which the original classifier made a false-positive prediction, but it might still make a false-negative prediction on the data over which the original classifier made a true prediction. This assumption can be written as:

$$(\text{PP})_o \Rightarrow (\text{PT})_t$$
$$(\text{PT})_o \Rightarrow (\text{PN})_t. \tag{6.17}$$

Tuning improves performance, when the misclassification cost decreases. We consider the benefit of tuning B_t to be the change in misclassification cost: If tuning corrects a false prediction, then we shall say that it gains benefit $(+1)$; if tuning incorrectly changes a formerly true prediction, it loses benefit (-1). For any general sequence of prediction results $\ldots \{\text{P}\}^l\{\text{N}\}^i\{\text{T}\}^j\ldots$ where $l > 0$, $i, j >= 0$ and $i + j > 0$,

(i) If $l = 1$ and $i \neq 0$, then $(\text{PN})_o => (\text{PN})_t$, tuning will be performed on a false-negative prediction, and tuning neither gains nor loses benefit.

(ii) If $l = 1$ and $i = 0$, but $j \neq 0$, then $(\text{PT})_o => (\text{PN})_t$, tuning loses benefit (-1), and further tuning will be performed on a false-negative prediction.

(iii) If $l = 2$ and $i \neq 0$, then $(\text{PPN})_o => (\text{PTN})_t$, tuning gains benefit $(+1)$, and further tuning will be performed on a false-negative prediction.

(iv) If $l = 2$ and $i = 0$, but $j \neq 0$, then $(\text{PPT})_o => (\text{PTN})_t$, tuning neither gains nor loses benefit, and further tuning will be performed on a false-negative prediction.

(v) If $l = 3$ and $i \neq 0$, then $(\text{PPPN})_o => (\text{PTTN})_t$, tuning gains benefit $(+2)$, and further tuning will be performed on a false-negative prediction.

(vi) If $l = 3$ and $i = 0$, but $j \neq 0$, then $(\text{PPPT})_o => (\text{PTTN})_t$, tuning gains benefit $(+2)$, and further tuning will be performed on a false-negative prediction.

(vii) When $l > 3$, $(\{\text{P}\}^l)_o => (\text{P}\{\text{T}\}^{l-1})_t$, tuning gains benefit $(+ (l-1))$.

The total benefit of tuning on all false predictions is calculated by:

$$B_t = -\sum (\text{PT})_o + \sum (\text{PPN})_o + 2 \cdot \sum (\text{PPP})_o + \cdots$$
$$+ (l-1) \cdot \sum (\{\text{P}\}^l)_o + \cdots , \tag{6.18}$$

where $l > 3$ and $\Sigma(\ldots)_o$ is the count of pattern $(\ldots)$ in the sequence of prediction results of the original classifier. The total benefit of tuning depends on how many continuous false-positive predictions the original classifier made on the data set. Table 7.25 does not show the data for every pattern where the length of successive false-positive prediction sequences l is greater than or equal to 3. Therefore, we cannot apply Eq. (6.18) to evaluate the benefit of tuning. Compared to the large number of false-positive predictions shown in column "P#", the small number of false-negative predictions shown in column "N#" can safely be ignored. To estimate the benefit of tuning from the data in Table 7.25, we first transform Eq. (6.18) to:

$$\mathrm{B}_t = -\sum (\mathrm{PT})_o - \sum (\mathrm{PN})_o + 2 \cdot \sum (\mathrm{PPP})_o + \cdots$$

$$+ (l-1) \cdot \sum (\{\mathrm{P}\}^l)_o + \cdots, \tag{6.19}$$

where "$+\Sigma(\mathrm{PPN})_o$" is removed from Eq. (6.18) and "$-\Sigma(\mathrm{PN})_o$" is added. Then combine $(\mathrm{PT})_o$ and $(\mathrm{PN})_o$ to $(\mathrm{P})_o$

$$\mathrm{B}_t = -\sum (\mathrm{P})_o + 2 \cdot \sum (\mathrm{PPP})_o + \cdots + (l-1) \cdot \sum (\{\mathrm{P}\}^l)_o + \cdots, \tag{6.20}$$

Equation (6.20) can be rewritten as:

$$\mathrm{B}_t = -n_1 + \frac{2}{3} n_3 + \cdots + \frac{l-1}{l} n_l + \cdots, \tag{6.21}$$

where $l > 3$ and n_l is the number of false-positive predictions which are in the pattern $(\{\mathrm{P}\}^l)_o$. Obviously,

$$\mathrm{B}_t > -n_1 + \frac{2}{3}(n_3 + \cdots + n_l + \cdots). \tag{6.22}$$

The column titled "$l = 1$" shows the percentage of n_1, the number of false-positive predictions in the pattern $(\mathrm{P})_o$, among all false-positive predictions; the column titled "$l \geq 3$" shows the percentage of $n_3 + \cdots + n_l + \cdots$ among all false-positive predictions.

6.3.5. *Fuzzy prediction filter*

As we stated in Chapter 1, a well-known problem of intrusion detection systems is that the alarms from IDSs could overwhelm the system user easily. We argue that IDS should take account on the user's capability of dealing with the alarms as well as the alarms itself. The fuzzy prediction filter in our system pushes the most suspicious predictions to the system user to be verified. The amount of the predictions is adjusted adaptively to avoid overwhelming the system user.

6.3.5.1. *Preliminary of fuzzy logic theory*

Fuzzy logic theory is a theory to deal with fuzziness [88]. There exists fuzziness everywhere in our daily life. For example, we might say, "it is a good cake." However, it depends on individuals whether the cake is actually good or not. Someone may think it is sweet enough to be a good cake, but other may think that it is too sweet to be a good cake. In this example, the words "sweet" and "good" are imprecise. Although we can measure the amount of sugar in a cake, we couldn't precisely define the term "sweet" based on the amount of sugar which could be accepted by all of us. In intrusion detection domain, as we mentioned above that alarms from IDSs could overwhelm the system user easily. We could measure the amount of alarms that an IDS outputs during a certain period, such as a minute, an hour, or a day. However, we could not define a threshold to be accepted by all system users, such that when the amount is over it, the user will be overwhelmed, while the amount is less than it, the user will not be overwhelmed. To solve such fuzziness, we turn to fuzzy set theory.

Fuzzy set theory [122] is the fundament of fuzzy logic theory, which is an extension of conventional crisp set theory. Given a crisp set, say a set of students in computer science department, every student is either in this set or not depending on student's major. However, sometimes it is difficult to express a set in binary logic, for example, a set of good students B. Suppose we just use the GPA as the metric and define a characteristic function in Eq. (6.23).

$$f_B(x) = \begin{cases} 1 & \text{if } x \cdot GPA \in [4.0, 5.0] \\ 0 & \text{if } x \cdot GPA \notin [4.0, 5.0] \end{cases}. \qquad (6.23)$$

Here we assume the maximal GPA is 5.0. Obviously, those students whose GPA is just little lower than 4.0 will complain this function. Also we will feel some guilty that we do not classify those students whose GPA is 3.99 into the set, but treat students whose GPA is 4.0 as good students. Although we can decrease the minimal GPA to make more students happy, complaints always exist but from some other students. For such a case, it is better to define a fuzzy set other than a crisp set. Formally, a fuzzy set A on the universe X is defined by a membership function $M_A(x)$, where $M_A(x)$ is a real value bounded from 0 to 1. The membership value $M_A(x)$ represents the degree of x belonging to the fuzzy set A. We can define the membership function of the fuzzy set B of good students as following:

$$M_B(x) = \begin{cases} 1 & \text{if } x \cdot GPA \in [4.0, 5.0] \\ x \cdot GPA/5.0 & \text{if } x \cdot GPA \notin [4.0, 5.0] \end{cases}. \quad (6.24)$$

Now, all of students are happy, there are good students in some degree depending on their GPAs as long as the GPA is not equal to zero. We also feel comfortable because now it is much fair.

Although a membership function could be any function in theory as long as its range is between 0 and 1, usually they are triangular, trapezoidal, or Gaussian function [89]. In our system, all fuzzy sets are defined by trapezoidal membership function as shown in Fig. 6.10. The function shown in Fig. 6.10 can be defined mathematically by Eq. (6.25):

$$M(x) = \begin{cases} 0 & \text{if } x \notin [X1, X4] \\ \dfrac{x - X1}{X2 - X1} & \text{if } x \in [X1, X2) \\ 1 & \text{if } x \in [X2, X3] \\ \dfrac{X4 - x}{X4 - X3} & \text{if } x \in (X3, X4] \end{cases} \quad (6.25)$$

The fundamental operations of fuzzy set, such as union, intersection and complement, can be defined by operations on their membership functions as following:

$$union: M_{A \cup B}(x) = \max(M_A(x), M_B(x)) \quad (6.26)$$

$$intersection: M_{A \cap B}(x) = \min(M_A(x), M_B(x)) \quad (6.27)$$

$$complement: M_{\bar{A}}(x) = 1 - M_A(x). \quad (6.28)$$

Fuzzy control is the first successful application of fuzzy theory where fuzzy rules are applied to control a system. The workflow of a fuzzy control

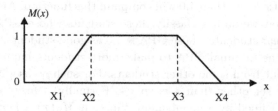

Fig. 6.10. Trapezoidal membership function.

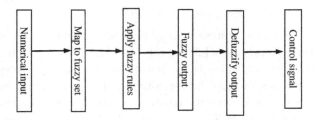

Fig. 6.11.   Workflow of fuzzy control system.

system is shown in Fig. 6.11. Fuzzy rules are described in nature language using fuzzy sets in IF-THEN form. For example, "IF a student's GPA, x, is high (A_i) THEN the student, y is good (B_j)", where A could be a fuzzy set with three elements {low, middle, high} on GPA, and B could be another fuzzy set with three elements {weak, fine, good} on student. A fuzzy output can be generated from fuzzy rule set given inputs through fuzzy reasoning.

In fuzzy reasoning procedure, the "PRODUCT-SUM" method [89] is used in our fuzzy controller. The output membership function for each rule is scaled (product) by the rule premise's degree of truth computed from the actual crisp input variables. The combined fuzzy output membership function is the sum of the output membership function from each rule.

$$M(x) = \sum_i (\alpha_i \times M_i(x)), \qquad (6.29)$$

where the $M_i(x)$ is the membership function of the conclusion in fuzzy rule i. The α_i is the rule's premise's degree of truth, which is computed by:

$$\alpha_i = \text{MIN}(M_1(x), M_2(x), \ldots). \qquad (6.30)$$

However, a fuzzy output usually will not be accepted as an actual control signal, a defuzzifier is needed to translate the fuzzy output to actual precise control signal. "CENTROID" defuzzification method [89] is used to finish this conversion, where the crisp value of the output variable is computed by finding the variable value of the center of gravity of the membership function for the fuzzy value. The center of gravity of the output membership function defined in Eq. (6.29) with respect to x is computed by:

$$m_c = \frac{\displaystyle\int_0^1 x \times M(x)dx}{\displaystyle\int_0^1 M(x)dx} = \frac{\displaystyle\sum_i \left(\alpha_i \times \int_0^1 x \times M_i(x)dx\right)}{\displaystyle\sum_i \left(\alpha_i \times \int_0^1 M_i(x)dx\right)}. \qquad (6.31)$$

6.3.5.2. *Motivation of fuzzy prediction filter*

An intrusion detection system usually generates alerts only when it finds some abnormal behaviors, while reports nothing to the system user when the input data are classified to be normal by the IDS. Correspondingly, there are two types of false: false-positive and false-negative. False alerts are false-positive. False-negative means that the IDS fail to detect a true intrusion. The value of IDS will be kept only if the system user performs defensive actions against actual intrusion. Obviously, it is desired for an intrusion detection system that the system user investigates and verifies very suspect predictions (or at least alerts) to keep the monitored system secure. However, it is impractical and inefficient due to the large amount of the alerts and the high false rate. To reduce false alerts, a common method is to check the correlation between the alerts and security information from other sources such as firewall, host configure, and application log. But correlation cannot eliminate all false alerts and does nothing on false-negative. Most available IDS products prioritize alerts in board level, such as critical, important, and unusual. The alert prioritizations help the system user to select the high priority alert to investigate and verify. But the system user has to manually filter some alerts according to the priority.

Doubtlessly, it costs the system user some time to investigate and verify one prediction. While the system user is verifying on a prediction, the IDS will continue making predictions on coming data. Some of them might be some very suspect predictions. A buffer is designated to hold those suspect predictions. There are two straight methods to design such a buffer. The first method is to set up a threshold of prediction suspicion, the buffer hold all predictions whose suspicions are greater than the threshold. This method doesn't take the system user into account and the buffered predictions could still overwhelm the system user in some case. The second method is to set up a threshold of the buffer length, the buffer won't hold more predictions than the threshold. This method reduces the pressure of the system user from the amount of predictions to be verified, but it takes the risk of missing some very suspect predictions after the length of the buffer reaches the threshold. A good solution should balance the desire to verify the most suspect predictions as many as possible while avoid overwhelming the system user. The buffer should be able to hold the most suspect predictions even if its length is long. On the other hand, when its length is short, the buffer should hold some predictions with lower suspicion. We may define a mathematic model which could balance the prediction suspicion and the buffer length to calculate whether a suspect prediction should be buffered. However, if we consider the system user when we define a mathematic model, it might be infeasible because the acceptable maximal length of the buffer depends on individuals. Obviously, there exists fuzziness on the terms such as short or long buffer. To balance the desire to verify suspect predictions as many as possible while avoid overwhelming the system user, we propose a fuzzy prediction filter to pick the most suspect predictions to the system user to verify in time while logging all predictions to be analyzed offline. Our fuzzy filter will consider the prediction suspicions and the buffer length dynamically.

6.3.5.3. *Input variable for fuzzy prediction filter*

The first step to build the fuzzy prediction filter is to determine the input variables. Because the filter is to pick up the most suspect predictions, we construct a variable to measure its uncertainty of every prediction from comprehensive elements. The first element is the prediction confidence. From previous discussion, we know every prediction has an associated prediction confidence ratio (PCR) to measure the degree that the prediction can be trusted to be true. On the other hand, the complement of the PCR measures the uncertainty of the prediction that it could be true, which could be part of prediction uncertainty. The second element is whether there is conflict among binary predictions when the final arbiter determines the final prediction. A final prediction is more trustable if it is picked out from non-conflictive binary predictions than picked out from conflictive binary predictions. These two factors are related to only one prediction on the data example. We still need to consider the performance on the past data. From Eq. (6.8) we know that the binary prediction engine sums up the confidence values of all rules that cover data, which means not all of rule could cover the same data. If we record whether a rule covers a data example for each rule, we get the coverage pattern. The third element is the performance of the coverage pattern on the past data. For each coverage pattern, it can be checked easily whether it was observed in the training data. For a new coverage pattern, it is safe to verify its prediction correctness even if it has high confidence ratio. For an observed coverage pattern, its false prediction rate on the training data set provides some degree of the prediction uncertainty. As our IDS running, model tuning will be executed on verified false predictions, some rules will be tuned while others keep unchanged (the detailed tuning algorithm will be introduced in the next subsection). The fourth element is the tuning frequency. We believe that if a rule keeps unchanged, most probably it is because the rule works well. While if a rule is tuned time to time, we think that this rule is not so stable, because every tuning is derived by false predictions. Therefore, the tuning frequency of a rule that covers the data example is also an important part of the prediction uncertainty. Put all these together, the prediction uncertainty (p_u) is determined by four factors: the complement of its PCR (c_{PCR}), the conflict factor (f_c) among the binary predictions, the false prediction rate (r_{fp}) of its coverage pattern, and the average tuning frequency (t_f) of all rules in its coverage pattern. Formally, a prediction uncertainty (p_u) could be defined by:

$$p_u = f_c \times \left(c_{PCR} + \frac{1}{2} \times r_{fp} + \frac{1}{2} \times \frac{1}{n} \times \sum_{i=1}^{n} t_{f_i} \right). \qquad (6.32)$$

After we construct the prediction uncertainty, we can pick up the most suspect prediction to system user easily. The next problem needs to be addressed is how many suspect predictions should be picked into a buffer. We think the buffer length couldn't completely indicate the capability of the system user. An experienced user can verify the same predictions more quickly than those inexperienced users. Of course, some predictions will cost a system user more time than others to verify due to the difficulty and complexity of investigation. The second variable of our fuzzy filter is estimated waiting time of a prediction (t_w), which is the product of the average verification time (t_v) on recently n verified predictions and the current buffer length (l_b):

$$t_w = \frac{1}{n} \times \left(\sum_{i=1}^{n} t_{vi} \right) \times l_b \qquad (6.33)$$

6.3.5.4. *Fuzzy knowledge base for fuzzy prediction filter*

Four fuzzy sets, such as "Low Uncertainty (LU)", "Average Uncertainty (AU)", "High Uncertainty (HU)" and "Extreme high Uncertainty (EU)", are defined for fuzzy input variable prediction uncertainty PU on its crisp value p_u shown in Fig. 6.11. Four other fuzzy sets, such as "Short Waiting (SW)", "Average Waiting (AW)", "Long Waiting (LW)" and "Extreme long Waiting (EW)", are defined for the fuzzy input variable estimated waiting time WT on its crisp value t_w shown in Fig. 6.12.

We use a term called filterable degree to measure the degree of a prediction to be filtered out. Three fuzzy sets, such as "Light Filtering (LF)", "Moderate Filtering (MF)" and "Strong Filtering (SF)", are defined

```
# 11 fuzzy sets for fuzzy prediction filter
(0)    Short Waiting (SW): (–, 0, 10, 20)
(1)    Average Waiting (AW): (10, 20, 30, 40)
(2)    Long Waiting (LW): (30, 40, 50, 60)
(3)    Extreme Long Waiting (EW): (50, 100, INF, –)

(4)    Low Uncertainty (LU): (–, 0, 0.1, 0.2)
(5)    Average Uncertainty (AU): (0.2, 0.4, 0.6, 0.8)
(6)    High Uncertainty (HU): (0.6, 0.8, 1.0, 1.5)
(7)    Extreme High Uncertainty (EU): (1.0, 1.5, 2.0, 2.0)

(8)    Light Filtering (LF): (–, 0, 0.1, 0.4)
(9)    Moderate Filtering (MF): (0.3, 0.5, 0.5, 0.7)
(10)   Strong Filtering (SF): (0.6, 0.9, 1.0, –)
```

Fig. 6.12.   Definitions of fuzzy set for fuzzy prediction filter.

```
# Total 16 fuzzy rules for fuzzy prediction filter
(11)   If the estimated waiting time (WT) is long (LW) and the prediction uncertainty
       (PU) is high (HU), and then the filtering degree (FD) for this prediction should be
       moderate (MF).
(12)   If the estimated waiting time (WT) is long (LW) and the prediction uncertainty
       (PU) is extreme high (EU), and then the filtering degree (FD) for this prediction
       should be light (LF).
(15)   If the estimated waiting time (WT) is extreme long (EW) and the prediction
       uncertainty (PU) is high (HU), and then the filtering degree (FD) for this
       prediction should be moderate (MF).
(16)   If the estimated waiting time (WT) is extreme long (EW) and the prediction
       uncertainty (PU) is extreme high (EU), and then the filtering degree (FD) for this
       prediction should be light (LF).
```

Fig. 6.13.   Some examples of fuzzy rules for fuzzy prediction filter.

for the fuzzy output variable filterable degree (FD) on its crisp value d_f shown in Fig. 6.12.

A total of 16 fuzzy rules are defined for fuzzy prediction filter. Some fuzzy rules are shown in Fig. 6.13.

6.3.5.5. *An example of fuzzy reasoning*

Record #90554 in test data was predicted to be an R2L attack in our system. The final prediction pattern was 0x8000000000004100. The estimated waiting time t_w in the buffer is 55, and the prediction uncertainty p_u is 1.224612. The goal of the fuzzy inference is to calculate the degree of this prediction to be filtered out.

Step 1: Calculate the degree of membership to every fuzzy set for the two crisp variables t_w and p_u, respectively, according to the definition of membership functions.

The results are:

$$M_{SW}(t_w) = 0, \quad M_{AW}(t_w) = 0, \quad M_{LW}(t_w) = 0.5,$$
$$M_{EW}(t_w) = 0.1, \quad M_{LU}(p_u) = 0, \quad M_{AU}(p_u) = 0,$$
$$M_{HU}(p_u) = 0.550776, \quad M_{EU}(p_u) = 0.449224.$$

Step 2: Calculate the rule's premise's degree of truth α_i for each rule by Eq. (6.5).

The results are:

$$\alpha_1 \ldots \alpha_{10} = 0, \quad \alpha_{11} = 0.5, \quad \alpha_{12} = 0.449224,$$
$$\alpha_{13} = 0, \quad \alpha_{14} = 0, \quad \alpha_{15} = 0.1, \quad \alpha_{16} = 0.1.$$

Step 3: Combine fuzzy output membership function from each fuzzy rule by Eq. (6.4):

$$M_O(d_f) = \alpha_{11} \times M_{MF}(d_f) + \alpha_{12} \times M_{SF}(d_f)$$
$$+ \alpha_{15} \times M_{MF}(d_f) + \alpha_{16} \times M_{SF}(d_f)$$
$$= 0.6 \times M_{MF}(d_f) + 0.549224 \times M_{SF}(d_f).$$

The definition of $M_{MF}(d_f)$ and $M_{SF}(d_f)$ in our system are:

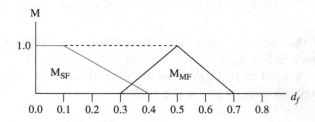

$$M_{MF}(d_f) = \begin{cases} 0 & d_f < 0.3 \text{ or } d_f > 0.7 \\ \dfrac{d_f - 0.3}{0.5 - 0.3} & 0.3 \le d_f \le 0.5 \\ \dfrac{0.7 - d_f}{0.7 - 0.5} & 0.5 \le d_f \le 0.7 \end{cases}$$

$$M_{SF}(d_f) = \begin{cases} 0 & d_f > 0.4 \\ 1 & 0 < d_f \le 0.1 \\ \dfrac{0.4 - d_f}{0.4 - 0.1} & 0.1 \le d_f \le 0.4 \end{cases}.$$

We get:

$$M_O(d_f) = \begin{cases} 0.549224 & 0 < d_f \le 0.1 \\ 0.549224 \times \dfrac{0.4 - d_f}{0.4 - 0.1} & 0.1 \le d_f \le 0.3 \\ 0.6 \times \dfrac{d_f - 0.3}{0.5 - 0.3} + 0.549224 & \\ \qquad \times \dfrac{0.4 - d_f}{0.4 - 0.1} & 0.3 \le d_f \le 0.4 \\ 0.6 \times \dfrac{d_f - 0.3}{0.5 - 0.3} & 0.4 \le d_f \le 0.5 \\ 0.6 \times \dfrac{0.7 - d_f}{0.7 - 0.5} & 0.5 \le d_f \le 0.7 \\ 0 & d_f > 0.7 \end{cases}.$$

Step 4: Defuzzify the fuzzy output by Eq. (6.6):

$$\int_0^1 M_O(x)\,dx$$

$$= 0.549224 \times \left(\int_0^{0.1} dx + \int_{0.1}^{0.4} \frac{0.4 - x}{0.4 - 0.1}\,dx \right) + 0.6$$

$$\times \left(\int_{0.3}^{0.5} \frac{x - 0.3}{0.5 - 0.3}\,dx + \int_{0.5}^{0.7} \frac{0.7 - x}{0.7 - 0.5}\,dx \right)$$

$$= 0.549224 \times \left(x \Big|_0^{0.1} + \frac{0.4x - 0.5x^2}{0.3} \Big|_{0.1}^{0.4} \right) + 0.6$$

$$\times \left(\frac{0.5x^2 - 0.3x}{0.2} \Big|_{0.3}^{0.5} + \frac{0.7x - 0.5x^2}{0.2} \Big|_{0.5}^{0.7} \right)$$

$$= 0.549224 \times (0.1 + 0.15) + 0.6 \times (0.1 + 0.1)$$

$$= 0.257306$$

$$\int_0^1 x \times M_O(x)dx$$

$$= 0.549224 \times \left(\int_0^{0.1} x dx + \int_{0.1}^{0.4} x \times \frac{0.4 - x}{0.4 - 0.1} dx \right) + 0.6$$

$$\times \left(\int_{0.3}^{0.5} x \times \frac{x - 0.3}{0.5 - 0.3} dx + \int_{0.5}^{0.7} x \times \frac{0.7 - x}{0.7 - 0.5} dx \right)$$

$$= 0.549224 \times \left(\frac{x^2}{2} \Big|_0^{0.1} + \frac{\frac{0.4}{2}x^2 - \frac{1}{3}x^3}{0.3} \Big|_{0.1}^{0.4} \right) + 0.6$$

$$\times \left(\frac{\frac{1}{3}x^3 - \frac{0.3}{2}x^2}{0.2} \Big|_{0.3}^{0.5} + \frac{\frac{0.7}{2}x^2 - \frac{1}{3}x^3}{0.2} \Big|_{0.5}^{0.7} \right)$$

$$= 0.549224 \times (0.005 + 0.03) + 0.6 \times (0.0433 + 0.0566)$$

$$= 0.07916284.$$

The degree of this prediction to be filtered out:

$$d_f = 0.07916284/0.257306 = 0.30766.$$

Since the threshold for the prediction filter is 0.5, so this prediction will not be filtered out and put into the suspicious prediction queue to be verified by the user.

6.3.6. *Fuzzy tuning controller*

We have introduced our model tuning algorithm in section 6.3.4.2 which could automatically tune the detection model on the fly according to the feedback provided by the system operator when false predictions were identified. But the user can only control whether the tuning should be performed by sending or blocking feedbacks on the false predictions. Furthermore, the tuning is automatically done with the same tuning degree, which is lack of refinement. To give the user more powerful but intuitive control on tuning the model, we developed a fuzzy tuning controller, so the user can tune the model fuzzily but yield much appropriate tuning by defining the fuzzy knowledge base through intuitive graphical user interface and/or familiar nature language.

6.3.6.1. *Motivation for fuzzy tuning controller*

As we discuss the basic model tuner in previous sections, the updating of the confidences is done after the user identifies a false prediction, and the tuned classifier will not be used to predict the data again which the original classifier just makes false prediction, so it depends on the subsequent data whether tuning could reduce falser predictions. Given any p and q where $p < 1$, $q > 1$, since the confidence of default rule is unchanged, trivially, there exists a number n, after updates the confidences n times continuously, the sign of the sum of confidences of all rules (positive rules and default rule) will be changed. That means the tuned classifier could make true prediction on the data that the original classifier makes false prediction on. Formally, $\exists n, (\{P\}^{n+1})_o => (P)_o(\{P\}^{n-1}T)_t, \exists m, (\{N\}^{m+1})_o => (N)_o(\{N\}^{m-1}T)_t$ where $(..)_o$ represents the sequence of prediction results of original classifier and $(..)_t$ stands for the sequence of prediction results of tuned classifier. Obviously, for a long sequence of subsequent false predictions, the lower p or greater q is, the smaller n and m will be, and the more false predictions the tuning could reduce. Of course, if the next data is such data that the original classifier makes true prediction, the tuning triggered by the last false prediction might be negative that the tuned classifier makes false prediction on the data, i.e., $(PT)_o => (P)_o(N)_t$ or $(NT)_o => (N)_o(P)_t$. In this case, the lower p or greater q is, the higher risk of negative tuning there exists. Unfortunately, the subsequent data are unknown future data to the model tuner. Thus it is almost impossible to work out the best p and q to reduce the false predictions as much as possible.

6.3.6.2. *Input variable for fuzzy tuning controller*

Although the subsequent data are unknown future data to the model tuner, the prediction confidence of the false prediction is known to the model tuner. We have some guideline to select p and q to achieve better performance. In general, if the magnitude of prediction confidence is high, p could be low or q could be great to reduce more false predictions meanwhile try to lower the risk of negative tuning. Correspondingly, if the magnitude of prediction confidence is low, p could be high or q could be low. Our first fuzzy input variable for the fuzzy tuning controller is prediction confidence ratio (PCR) instead of prediction confidence (PC).

We know that it costs the system user some time to investigate and verify one prediction. Assume the user takes t intervals of coming data to identify the false prediction, and then these t subsequent data will be still predicted by the original classifier. Unfortunately, it is impractical to know how many true predictions the original classifiers could make on those t subsequent data before the model tuner tunes the model, because the user just finishes verifying one false prediction. However, the binary

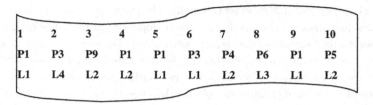

1	2	3	4	5	6	7	8	9	10
P1	P3	P9	P1	P1	P3	P4	P6	P1	P5
L1	L4	L2	L2	L1	L1	L2	L3	L1	L2

Fig. 6.14.   Sliding window holding coverage patterns and predicted labels.

prediction engine can keep track on the coverage pattern at least for subsequent data in a slide window and pass them to the corresponding model tuner. Furthermore, the final predicted labels on all those subsequent data are available when the model tuner is ready to tune the model as shown in Fig. 6.14, where the first line is the data record number, and the second line is the coverage pattern, and the third line is predicted label. In Fig. 6.14, the right row (10, P5, L2) is the newest entry of the slide window.

We can calculate two parameters on these stored data given a coverage pattern and its predicted label and actual label, for example, coverage pattern P1 and predicted label L1 but the actual label is L2 on a data record. The corresponding coverage pattern and predicted label could be found in the slide window (e.g., the left one (1, P1, L1)), or had been slid out from the slide window. The first is the cover rate, the percentage of given coverage pattern in the slide window, in our example, the coverage rate is 0.4 because there are four entries whose coverage pattern is P1. The higher cover rate indicates that the tuning will affect more predictions.

The final predicted labels are determined by final arbiter, and they could be different although their coverage patterns are same for a particular binary classifier because the final arbiter picks the prediction results from different binary classifiers. The percentage of predictions with the same coverage pattern and final predicted label over all predictions with same coverage pattern is the false rate. For the given coverage pattern P1, predicted label L1 and actual label L2 in our example, the false rate is 0.75 because there are three entries whose coverage pattern is P1 and predicted label is L1. The higher false rate requires more aggressive tuning. We define false cover rate r_{fc} by the product of the cover rate and false rate and use the false cover rate as our second input variable in our revised fuzzy tuning controller. In our example, the false cover rate is 0.3 (0.4*0.75).

6.3.6.3. *Fuzzy knowledge base for fuzzy tuning controller*

Four fuzzy sets, such as "Low Prediction Confidences Ratio" (*LPCR*), "Average Prediction Confidences Ratio" (*APCR*), "High Prediction Confidences Ratio" (*HPCR*), and "Extreme high Prediction Confidences Ratio" (*EPCR*), are defined for the input variable prediction confidence ratio *PCR* on the crisp variable r_{pc}.

Four fuzzy sets, such as "Low False Coverage Rates" (*LFCR*), "Average False Coverage Rates" (*AFCR*), "High False Coverage Rates" (*HFCR*), and "Extreme high False Coverage Rates" (*EFCR*), are defined for the input variable false cover rate *FCR* on the crisp variable r_{fc}.

Three fuzzy sets, such as "Slight Tuning" (*ST*), "Moderate Tuning" (*MT*), and "Aggressive Tuning" (*AT*), are defined for a fuzzy output variable *TD* for tuning strength on the crisp variable S_t (Fig. 6.15).

A total of 16 fuzzy rules for fuzzy tuning controller are defined. Some rules are shown in Fig. 6.16.

#11 Fuzzy sets for fuzzy tuning controller
(0)   Low Prediction Confidence Ratio (LPCR): (0.0001, 0.01, 0.05, 0.2)
(1)   Average Prediction Confidence Ratio (APCR): (0.05, 0.2, 0.4, 0.6)
(2)   High Prediction Confidence Ratio (HPCR): (0.4, 0.6, 0.7, 0.9)
(3)   Extreme high Prediction Confidence Ratio (EPCR): (0.7, 0.9, 1.0, –)
(4)   Low False Coverage Rate (LFCR): (–, 0, 0.005, 0.01)
(5)   Average False Coverage Rate (AFCR): (0.005, 0.01, 0.04, 0.1)
(6)   High False Coverage Rate (HFCR): (0.04, 0.1, 0.15, 0.2)
(7)   Extreme high False Coverage Rate (EFCR): (0.15, 0.5, 1.0, –)
(8)   Aggressive Tuning (AT): (–INF, 0, 0.1, 0.5)
(9)   Moderate Tuning (MT): (0.1, 0.5, 0.5,0.9)
(10)   Slight Tuning (ST): (0.5, 0.9, 1.0, –)

Fig. 6.15.   Definitions of fuzzy sets for fuzzy tuning controller.

---

(1)   If prediction confidence ratio (PCR) is low (LPCR) and false coverage rate (FCR) is low (LFCR), and then tuning degree (TD) should be slight (ST).
(4)   If prediction confidence ratio (PCR) is low (LPCR) and false coverage rate (FCR) is extreme high (EFCR), and then tuning degree (TD) should be moderate (MT).
(9)   If prediction confidence ratio (PCR)is high (HPCR) and false coverage rate (FCR) is low (LFCR), and then tuning degree (TD) should be moderate (MT).
(14) If prediction confidence ratio (PCR) is extreme high (EPCR) and false coverage rate (FCR) is average (AFCR), and then tuning degree (TD) should be aggressive (AT).

Fig. 6.16.   Examples of fuzzy rules for fuzzy tuning control.

Chapter 7

System Prototype and Performance Evaluation

7.1. Implementation of Prototype

7.1.1. *Fuzzy controller*

The operation GetOutput() shown in Fig. 7.1 implements Eqs. (6.7)–(6.9). The retuned value is corresponding to m_c in Eqs. (6.7)–(6.9).

7.1.2. *Binary prediction and model tuning thread*

To access the detection model exclusively, the binary prediction engine and model tuner in our ADAT intrusion detection system were implemented in the same thread as shown in Fig. 7.2. There are five such threads, one for each binary classifier. When the binary prediction is made on a received data record, its coverage pattern is constructed and kept in the *myCoverSlidingWindow*. The predicted label of this data record will be set after the final arbiter gets it as shown in Fig. 7.2. The object *myTuningSlidingWindow* handles coverage pattern whose corresponding rules were tuned. The average tuning frequency t_f is sent to final arbiter and prediction filter thread to calculate the prediction uncertainty.

When the coverage pattern is ready to tune, its cover rate and false rate on the slide window are calculated, which will be used by *myFuzzyTuningController* with prediction confidence ratio (PCR) to get the tuning strength d_t. Then the rules in the coverage pattern will be tuned by calling the member function TuneModel of the object *myDetectionModel*. This coverage pattern will be put into *myTuningSlideWindow* to update related rules' average tuning frequency.

101

```
float CFuzzyController::GetOutput(float x,float y)
{
  CFuzzyRule *pRule;
float fIntegralZMZ = 0, fIntegralMZ = 0;

for (POSITION Pos = m_pRuleList.GetHeadPosition(); Pos != NULL;){
     pRule = (CFuzzyRule *) m_pRuleList.GetNext(Pos) ;
     fIntegralMZ += pRule→GetIntegralMZ(x,y);
     fIntegralZMZ += pRule→GetIntegralZMZ(x,y);
  }
  return fIntegralZMZ/fIntegralMZ ;
}
```

Fig. 7.1.   Pseudo code to implement the fuzzy reasoning procedure.

```
LOOP
   ReceiveNewData(&Data);
   if (Data.Type == input_data)
     BinaryPredictionResult = myDetectionModel.PredictData(Data);
     myCoverSlidingWindow.AddPattern(Data.CoveragePattern);
     t_f = myTuningSlidingWindow.GetAvgTuningFrequency(Data.CoveragePattern);
     SendBinaryPredictionResult2FinalArbiter(Data, BinaryPredictionResult, t_f);
   else   /* Data.Type == feedback_data */
     r_pc = Data.PredicitonConfidenceRatio;
     r_c = myCoverSlidingWindow.GetCoverRate(Data.CoveragePattern);
     r_f = myCoverSlidingWindow.GetFalseRate(Data.CoveragePattern,
Data.PredictedLabel)
     d_t = myFuzzyTuningController.GetOutput(r_pc, r_f*r_c); // calculate tuning strength
     myDetectionModel.TuneModel(Data.CoveragePattern, d_t);
     myTuningSlidingWindow.AddPattern(Data.CoveragePattern);
END
```

Fig. 7.2.   Pseudo code for prediction/tuning thread.

7.1.3. *Final arbiter and prediction filter thread*

The fuzzy filter was implemented in the final arbiter thread. This thread arbitrates binary predictions to get the final result first. Every prediction is logged to support possible offline analysis. After calculating the filtering degree, the suspect prediction with low filtering degree will be send to verification thread (Fig. 7.3).

7.1.4. *User simulator thread*

A verification thread was implemented to simulate the users who verify the prediction results. The goal of the verification thread in our prototype is

```
LOOP
    CollectAllBinaryPredictions(&Data);
    Data.PredLabel = myFinalArbiter.ArbitratePredicitons(Data);
    myCoverSlideWindow.SetPredLabel(Data.Pattern, Data.PredLabel);
    LogFinalPrediction(Data, Data.PredLabel);

    tw = GetEstimatedWaitingTime();
    pu = CaculatePredictionUncertainty(Data);
    fd = myFuzzyPredictionFilter.GetOutput(tw, pu);
    if (fd < threshold ) SendSuspectPredictiontoVerify(Data);
End
```

Fig. 7.3.   Pseudo code for final arbiter/prediction filtering thread.

to put some randomly delay before model tuner gets the feedback on false predictions. In our experiments, the random delay is limited between 0.5 and 3 minutes.

7.1.5. *Interface for fuzzy knowledge base*

Our fuzzy knowledge base is stored in a plain text file, and the initial setting of the fuzzy sets and fuzzy rules is edited directly in text mode. The fuzzy knowledge base also can be viewed and updated intuitively through a dialog as shown in Fig. 7.4 while the system is running. The graph of membership function of selected fuzzy set is shown along with its four parameters. The user can change the function by setting new parameters. The selected fuzzy rule is also viewable and can be modified by selecting new available fuzzy sets for fuzzy input variables or output variable. Before the modification is taken effective, the user can test the fuzzy controller by inputting the crisp variables and checking the crisp output value.

7.2. Experimental Data set and Related Systems

7.2.1. *KDDCup'99 intrusion detection data set*

A proper data set must be obtained to facilitate experimentation and performance evaluation. In our experimental environment, it was difficult to obtain real-life data sets due to limitations of network size and limited external access. Unfortunately, usable data sets are rarely published as these involve sensitive information, such as the network architecture, security mechanisms, and so on. Thus, in our research we rely on the publicly

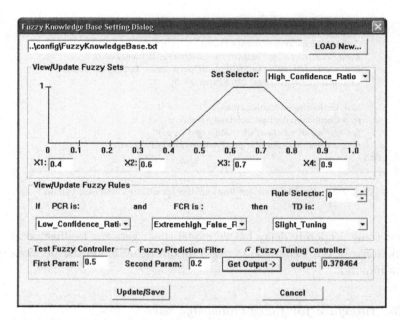

Fig. 7.4.   Graphical user interface for fuzzy knowledge base.

available KDDCup'99 intrusion detection data set. This data set was collected from a network simulating a typical U.S. Air Force LAN and also reflects dynamic change within the network. The detailed description of KDDCup'99 contest can be found at http://kdd.ics.uci.edu/databases/ kddcup99/task.html. The data set is available at http://kdd.ics.uci.edu/ databases/kddcup99/kddcup99.html. Here we give brief introduction on the data set.

The KDDCup'99 intrusion detection data set was developed based on the 1998 DARPA intrusion detection evaluation program, prepared and managed by MIT Lincoln Labs. The objective of this program was to survey and evaluate intrusion detection research. Lincoln Labs set up an environment to acquire nine weeks of raw TCP data for a local-area network (LAN) simulating a typical U.S. Air Force LAN. This LAN was operated as if a true Air Force environment, and it was subjected to multiple attacks. The raw training data dump was about four gigabytes of compressed binary TCP data from the first seven weeks of network traffic alone. The data dump was processed into roughly five million connection records. The test data were constructed from the network traffic in the last two weeks, which yielded around two million connection records. Each record represents a TCP/IP network connection with a total of 41 attributes (features). Domain experts derive some of the features related to content. Some statistic features are generated using two seconds time window. Five classes of connections were identified, including normal and abnormal (attack) network connections. The four classes of attacks are denial-of-service (DOS), probing (PROBE), remote-to-local (R2L), and user-to-root (U2R). Each attack class is further divided into some subclasses. For example, class "DOS" includes subclass "smurf", "neptune", "back", "teardrop", and so on, representing popular types of denial-of-service attacks.

Two training data sets from the first seven weeks of network traffic are available. The full data set includes about five million records, and a smaller subset containing only 10% of the data records but with the same distribution as the full data set. The labeled test data set includes 311,029 records, but distribution of attacks is different from the training data set (see Table 7.1). Further, 17 out of 38 types of attack in the test data are not present in the training data set. The different distributions between the training data set and test data set and the new types of attacks in the test data set reflect the dynamic change of the nature of attacks common in real-life systems. Sabhnani and Serpen analyzed the dissimilarity between the training data set and test data set [69].

7.2.2. *Performance evaluation method*

As interest in intrusion detection has grown, more attentions pay to evaluation of IDSs. Performance evaluation of a system is quite important to improve itself. When an IDS is reported, usually its individual performance evaluation result will be reported, but lack of comparisons with other systems. Different IDSs can use varied detection approaches on distinct data. Evaluating an IDS and comparing it with other IDSs is a difficult task due to the availability of high-quality data/attacks, network privacy, and competitive issues. The performance of IDSs can be measured in different aspects, such as detection rate, false alarm rate as well as the cost of misclassification.

Table 7.1. Data distribution in the KDDCup'99 ID data set.

	Normal (%)	PROBE (%)	DOS (%)	U2R (%)	R2L (%)
Training data set	19.69	0.83	79.24	0.01	0.23
Test data set	19.48	1.34	73.90	0.07	5.21

7.2.2.1. *Standard basic metrics*

The goal of IDSs is to detect intrusion completely and accurately, and there are two kinds of errors corresponding, namely false-negative and false-positive results. If IDSs simply classify activities into normal or intrusion, the follow standard metrics can be used to evaluate their performance.

Based on Table 7.2, more terms can be defined as follows:

$$\text{Precision} = \text{TP}/(\text{TP} + \text{FP})$$

$$\text{Recall} = \text{TP}/(\text{TP} + \text{FN}) \tag{7.1}$$

$$\text{F-value} = \frac{(1 + \beta^2) \times \text{Recall} \times \text{Precision}}{\beta^2 \times \text{Recall} + \text{Precision}}.$$

The precision measures that how many percent of reported intrusions are true intrusions, meanwhile the recall measures that how many percent of actual intrusions are reported. The importance of recall is obvious, because any undetected intrusion is quite dangerous to system. But the precision is also quite important to an IDS, because each alarm will cost operator some time to analyze it. If an IDS generate too many false-positive alarms, the alarms including the true-positive alarms will be ignored totally by the operator due to the overload analysis.

7.2.2.2. *Receiver operating characteristic (ROC) analysis*

Most of the IDSs have some adjustable threshold or other parameters, for example, the statistical threshold in statistical analysis, the command length in neural network, the support, and confidence in data mining-based method. In such systems, the detection rate and the false alarm rate are dependent on these adjustable parameters. The receiver operating characteristic (ROC) curve (see example in Fig. 7.5) can be used to plot the true-positive rate against the false-positive rate by tuning those internal parameters. The ROC curve can also be used not only to compare the performance on different systems but also to select the optimal parameter values for each system.

Table 7.2.   Standard metrics for evaluations of IDSs.

Standard metrics		Classified activity by an IDS	
		Normal	Intrusion
Actual activity	Normal	True negative (TN)	False positive (FP)
	Intrusion	False negative (FN)	True positive (TP)

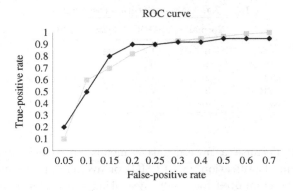

Fig. 7.5.   Example of ROC curve.

7.2.2.3. *Confusion matrix*

The attack can be classified into different categories, such as denial-of-service (DOS), probing (PROBE), remote attacks (R2L), and local user attacks (U2R). Each category can be further identified into different subclasses. For example, smurf, netpune, back, teardrop, and pod are some types of DOS attack.

Modern IDSs will associate the possible intrusion attack type to each alarm to help verify it easily. Of course, correct attack type association is helpful, but wrong type will mislead the verification. To evaluate the performance on multiple classes, an m-by-m confusion matrix (shown in Table 7.3) may be constructed, in which m is the number of classes. Each entry in this confusion matrix $\mathrm{CM}(x, y)$ is the number of test records which actually belong to class x but are predicted into class y.

A misclassification cost matrix (shown in Table 7.4) can also be constructed in similar way. Each entry $C(x, y)$ is the cost for each misclassification from class x to class y. The misclassification cost matrix is usually not symmetric. Especially the cost between normal and attacks

Table 7.3.   Example of confusion matrix.

	Normal	PROBE	DOS	U2R	R2L
Normal	60,315	213	55	3	7
PROBE	150	3,881	135	0	0
DOS	5,966	244	223,566	4	73
U2R	21	135	1	68	3
R2L	14,189	173	1	279	1,547

Table 7.4.   Misclassification cost matrix.

	Normal	PROBE	DOS	U2R	R2L
Normal	0	1	2	2	2
PROBE	1	0	2	2	2
DOS	2	1	0	2	2
U2R	3	2	2	0	2
R2L	4	2	2	2	0

is directional because a false-negative means an attack is undetected. The totally misclassification cost (TMC) or average misclassification cost (AMC) can be computed for easily measuring the performance from the confusion matrix and misclassification cost matrix.

$$TMC = \sum_{x,y} CM(x,y) \times C(x,y),$$

$$AMC = \frac{TMC}{\sum_{x,y} CM(x,y)}.$$

(7.2)

7.2.3. *Related IDSs on KDDCup'99 ID data set*

Sabhnani and Serpen (2003) evaluated the performance of a comprehensive set of pattern recognition and machine learning algorithms on KDDCup'99 ID data set in [69]. Those algorithms include multi-layer perceptron, Gaussian classifier, K-means clustering, nearest cluster algorithm, incremental radial basis function, leader algorithm, hyper-sphere algorithm, fuzzy ARTMAP, and C4.5 decision tree. The evaluation results showed that there is no single algorithm that could detect all attack categories with a high probability of detection and a low false alarm rate. However, for a given attack category, certain algorithm demonstrates superior detection performance compared to others. Based on this finding a multi-classifier model was proposed [70]. Each sub-classifier in the model was trained using the algorithm which has the best performance for the given attack category. Multi-layer perceptron was chosen for "PROBE" attack; K-means was chosen for "DOS" and "U2R" attack; and Gaussian was chosen for "R2L". The multi-classifier model got better performance on the test data set: the total misclassification cost is 71,096, and the cost per example is 0.2285. Detailed results [70] are shown in Table 7.5. Although it gets the better performance, the significant drawback is that this multi-classifier model was built based on the performance of different sub-classifiers on the test

Table 7.5. Detailed prediction results on test data set of MLMTA.

	Normal	PROBE	DOS	U2R	R2L	Accuracy (%)
Normal	60,315	213	55	3	7	99.54
PROBE	150	3,881	135	0	0	93.16
DOS	5,966	244	223,566	4	73	97.26
U2R	21	135	1	68	3	29.82
R2L	14,189	173	1	279	1,547	9.56
FP-rate	25.21%	16.47%	0.09%	80.79%	5.09%	

Total misclassification cost = 71,096, false-negative rate = 8.12%

data set. Usually, the test data set should not be used during the procedure to build a classifier model.

Giacinto *et al.* (2003) proposed a multiple classifier system for intrusion detection based on distinct feature representations [74]. These classifiers were trained on certain features of training data set instead of all available features. In this point, this design of those classifiers is quite different with others. Three groups of features: content features, intrinsic features, and traffic features were used, respectively, to train three classifiers, and then a decision fusion function was used to generate the final prediction. The 10% subset of KDDCup'99 training data set was used to train the classifiers, and the performance on the entire test data set was evaluated. The cost per example is 0.2254. No confusion matrix of the prediction is reported. A modular multiple classifier system was also built for each network connection service, such as web, mail, ftp service, and so on. The cost per example was dropped to 0.1688 in their best result [74].

Kumar (2002) applied RIPPER to KDDCup'99 data set [71]. RIPPER is an optimized rule-learning algorithm to reduce error on large data set [72]. RIPPER was used to train a model on the 10% subset of the training data set, and tested on entire test set. The total misclassification cost is 73,622, and the cost per example is 0.2367, which is same as the third rank of the contest. Detailed results [73] are shown in Table 7.6.

Agarwal and Joshi (2001) proposed an improved two-stage general-to-specific framework (PNrule) of learning a rule-based model based on their original work in KDDCup'99 contest [75]. PNrule balances the support and accuracy when it is discovering rules from its training data set to overcome the problem of small disjuncts. For multi-class classification problems, a cost-sensitive scoring algorithm was developed to resolve the conflicts among multiple classifiers using the misclassification cost matrix, and the final prediction was made according to Bayes optimality rule. PNrule was

Table 7.6.   Detailed prediction results on test data set of simple RIPPER.

	Normal	PROBE	DOS	U2R	R2L	Accuracy (%)
Normal	60,251	259	57	14	12	99.44
PROBE	894	3,085	187	0	0	74.05
DOS	6,291	281	223,281	0	0	97.14
U2R	212	0	1	9	6	3.95
R2L	14,600	0	4	4	1,581	9.77
FP-rate	26.74%	14.90%	0.11%	66.67%	1.13%	

Total misclassification cost = 73,622, false-negative rate = 8.78%

Table 7.7.   Detailed prediction results on test data set of PNrule.

	Normal	PROBE	DOS	U2R	R2L	Accuracy (%)
Normal	60,316	175	75	13	14	99.54
PROBE	889	3,042	26	3	206	73.02
DOS	6,815	57	222,874	106	1	96.96
U2R	195	3	0	15	15	6.58
R2L	14,440	12	1	6	1,730	10.69
FP-rate	27.03%	7.51%	0.046%	89.51%	12.00%	

Total misclassification cost = 74,058, false-negative rate = 8.92%

applied on KDDCup'99 ID data set. The total misclassification cost is 74,058, and the cost per example is 0.2381. Detailed results [76] are shown in Table 7.7. Although cost per example is between the third and fourth ranks of all contest results, PNrule has the highest detect accuracy of class "normal" and class "R2L" among our reviewed systems.

Pfahringer (2000) constructed an ensemble of 50×10 C5 decision trees as a final predictor using so-called cost-sensitive bagged boosting algorithm during KDDCup'99 contest [77]. The final prediction was made according to minimal conditional risk, which is a sum of error-cost time class-probabilities. Fifty specific samples were drawn from the original entire training data set. This predictor is the winner of the contest. The total misclassification cost is 72,500, and the cost per example is 0.2331. Detailed results [76] are shown in Table 7.8.

Levin (2000) proposed a data-mining tool called Kernel Miner based on building the optimal decision forest [78]. The tool won the second place in the KDDCup'99 contest. A global optimization criterion was used to minimize a value of the multiple estimators including the total cost of misclassifications. The available 10% subset of the training data set was used to build the decision forest. The total misclassification cost is 73,243,

Table 7.8. Detailed prediction results on test data set of contest winner.

	Normal	PROBE	DOS	U2R	R2L	Accuracy (%)
Normal	60,262	243	78	4	6	99.45
PROBE	511	3,471	184	0	0	83.32
DOS	5,299	1,328	223,226	0	0	97.12
U2R	168	20	0	30	10	13.16
R2L	14,527	294	0	8	1,360	8.40
FP-rate	25.39%	35.19%	0.12%	28.57%	1.16%	

Total misclassification cost = 72,500, false-negative rate = 8.19%

Table 7.9. Detailed prediction results on test data set of contest runner-up.

	Normal	PROBE	DOS	U2R	R2L	Accuracy (%)
Normal	60,244	239	85	9	16	99.42
PROBE	458	3,521	187	0	0	84.52
DOS	5,595	227	224,029	2	0	97.47
U2R	177	18	4	27	2	11.84
R2L	14,994	4	0	6	1,185	7.32
FP-rate	26.05%	12.17%	0.12%	38.64%	1.50%	

Total misclassification cost = 73,287, false-negative rate = 8.47%

and the cost per example is 0.2356. Detailed results [78] are shown in Table 7.9.

All of above proposed systems were designed and evaluated on KDDCup'99 data set, and test results at the least cost per example were reported. There are other intrusion detection systems that KDDCup'99 data set used but no comparable test result was reported. Below are brief overviews of such systems.

Ertoz *et al.* (2003) used shared nearest neighbor similarity and core points to find clusters in high-dimensional data [79], where the clusters are widely differing in shapes, sizes, and densities. KDDCup'99 data set was used to validate the performance. However, only the training data set was used in the experiments and no independent test data set was used to evaluate its performance.

Yeung and Chow (2002) proposed Parzen-window intrusion detectors [80], which use a non-parametric density estimation approach based on Parzen-windows estimators with Gaussian kernels. In this system, only normal data were used to train. Nevertheless, this model is just a binary classifier. A test example can only be classified into normal or attack.

Gomez and Dasgupta (2002) applied fuzzy logic and genetic algorithm to generate fuzzy rules of classifiers for intrusion detection [81]. An adaptive-parameter genetic algorithm (GA) with special operators (gene addition, gene deletion) was used to evolve fuzzy classifier for each class (normal and attack). Only the 10% subset of training data set was used in their experimentation.

7.3. Performance Evaluation

7.3.1. *SOM-based labeling tool performance*

We perform our experiments on KDDCup'99 ID 10% training data set. In this ID data set, nine out of forty-one features are symbolic. All training data are clustered into 210 sets according to the combined values of these three symbolic features. The set sizes varied greatly from 1 to 281,400. There is one set whose size is over 100,000. And three other sets have over 10,000 data records. A total of 182 sets have less than 100 data records, and 72 sets among them have less than 10 data records. All sets with over 100 data records are listed in Table 7.10.

There is no SOM to be trained for those 72 sets with less than 10 data records. The size of SOM is around 10% of amount of data records in a pre-clustered set. To limit training time on large pre-clustered data set, we restrict the largest SOM to 400 nodes even for the largest pre-clustered set. Table 7.11 shows the initial settings of SOM size in our experiments.

Table 7.10.   List of pre-clustered set with over 100 data records.

Protocol	Service	Flag	Amount	Protocol	Service	Flag	Amount
icmp	ecr_i	SF	281,400	tcp	Private	RSTR	477
tcp	private	S0	81,964	tcp	Finger	SF	467
tcp	http	SF	58,546	udp	ntp_u	SF	380
tcp	private	REJ	19,708	tcp	Other	RSTR	260
tcp	smtp	SF	9,566	tcp	telnet	SF	242
udp	private	SF	8,512	tcp	Other	S0	227
udp	domain_u	SF	5,863	tcp	Auth	SF	220
udp	other	SF	5,598	tcp	http	S0	200
tcp	http	REJ	5,354	tcp	Finger	S0	183
tcp	ftp_data	SF	4,534	tcp	telnet	S0	180
icmp	eco_i	SF	1,642	tcp	ftp_data	S0	154
tcp	other	REJ	1,081	tcp	Private	RSTO	113
tcp	ftp	SF	687	tcp	Smtp	S0	112
icmp	urp_i	SF	538	tcp	remote_job	S0	100

Table 7.11.   Initial setting of SOM size.

Pre-clustered set size	281,400–4,534	1,642–687	538–380	260–154	113–73	51–10
SOM size	20 × 20	10 × 10	7 × 7	4 × 4	3 × 3	2 × 2

Table 7.12.   Distribution of inputs with large distance for top 10 large data set.

Data set name	Size	Avg. distance	>0.01	>0.02	>0.03	>0.04	>0.05	>0.1
icmpecr_iSF	281,400	0.00001589	126	68	37	18	6	0
tcpprivateS0	81,964	0.00046957	219	100	73	51	41	25
tcphttpSF	58,546	0.00261334	2,908	1,558	979	683	522	188
tcpprivateREJ	19,708	0.00048859	157	108	81	50	37	16
tcpsmtpSF	9,566	0.00785686	1,382	706	455	329	238	74
udpprivateSF	8,512	0.00094749	216	116	71	42	22	0
udpdomain_uSF	5,863	0.00556824	942	423	246	154	103	17
udpotherSF	5,598	0.00100146	128	43	12	3	0	0
tcphttpREJ	5,354	0.00574129	731	336	203	138	99	19
tcpftp_dataSF	4,534	0.00873741	879	474	314	220	158	26

In our experiments, 82 out of 138 average distances of pre-clustered data sets are less than 0.01, 107 out of 138 average distances of pre-clustered data sets are less than 0.02, and 127 out of 138 average distances of pre-clustered data sets are less than 0.1. After the label tool stopped training, we examine the distance distribution for each data set to train a larger SOM if necessary. Table 7.12 shows the distribution for the top 10 large data sets clustered by 400-node SOMs.

The right six columns record the number of inputs whose distances to their best matching nodes are greater than the specific values. For example, the entry of second row and fourth column is 126, which means there are 126 inputs whose distances to their best matching nodes are greater than 0.01. Compared to other rows, the third and fifth rows show that the clustering qualities on the data sets (tcphttpSF and tcpsmtpSF) are not good. We increased the size of SOMs and clustered the data sets again. The new results are shown in Table 7.13.

In our label tool, data clustered into different nodes by SOM, even adjective nodes, will not be grouped together to form a large cluster. For every node, if there is at least one input datum is clustered into this node, the input datum with minimal distance to the node is required to be labeled manually. If a large SOM is trained to cluster the data in a data set, the number of inputs to be labeled manually increases too. We stopped to train a larger SOM over 1,200 nodes for data set tcphttpSF to avoid labeling too much input data manually. The nodes number 900 is around 10% of the

Table 7.13. Distribution of inputs with large distance for data sets clustered by large SOMs.

Data set name	SOM size	Avg. distance	>0.01	>0.02	>0.03	>0.04	>0.05	>0.1
tcphttpSF	600	0.00188474	2,216	1,122	656	440	329	93
tcphttpSF	900	0.00149114	1,710	850	518	358	261	68
tcphttpSF	1,200	0.001304559	1,491	712	431	293	223	72
tcpsmtpSF	600	0.00609857	1,063	516	330	251	183	53
tcpsmtpSF	900	0.00449187	805	365	239	166	114	22

Table 7.14. Label results for top 10 large data sets.

Data set name	Verified data amount	Mislabeled data amount	SOM size
icmpecr_iSF.stat	305	12	400
tcpprivateS0.stat	423	0	400
tcphttpSF.stat	1,248	125	1,200
tcpprivateREJ.stat	431	0	400
tcpsmtpSF.stat	867	2	900
udpprivateSF.stat	295	7	400
udpdomain_uSF.stat	400	0	400
udpotherSF.stat	376	2	400
tcphttpREJ.stat	392	0	400
tcpftp_dataSF.stat	385	95	400

data set size 9,566 for data set tcpsmtpSF. For all other data sets clustered by SOMs whose size is less than 400, we didn't increase the size of SOM to cluster the data set again, since the SOM size is around of 10% of data set size (Table 7.11).

There are 6,111 (including 151 input data in those data sets whose size are less than 10) out of 494,021 input data in the KDDCup'99 10% training data set (about 1.2370%) which were verified and labeled manually. Only 328 (about 0.0664%) input data elements were mislabeled. The label results for top 10 large data sets are shown in Table 7.14.

7.3.2. *Build hybrid detection model*

The training data in KDDCup'99 data set includes examples with multiple class labels (total of 22 attack types plus "Normal"). However, the binary SLIPPER rule learning system only accepts training examples with two class labels. We built binary classifiers for "Normal" (BC-Normal) and attack categories (e.g., BC-DOS for DOS attacks) instead of attack types (e.g., smurf) as shown in Fig. 7.6.

To build each binary classifier, we need to preprocess the training data to get the right training data set $(T_N, T_P, T_D, T_U, T_R)$ for each positive

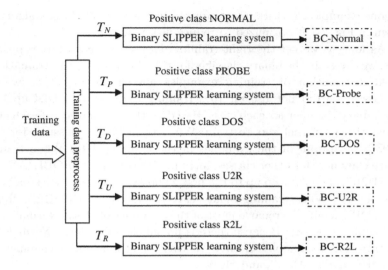

Fig. 7.6. System diagram to build binary classifiers.

Given: Training Set $T : \{(\ features_i, label_i)\}$, $i=1...N$, and Classes Set $C : \{(cname_j, counter_j, fname_j)\}$, $j=1...M$; where $label_i \in \{c.cname \mid c \in C\}$.

for each training example $t \in T$
for each class $c \in C$
if $t.label \neq c.cname$
    assign "other" to $t.label$
    $c.counter$ ++
    output t to $c.fname$
restore $t.label$

Fig. 7.7. Optimized preprocess algorithm.

class respectively. The preprocess procedure is very simple, as described in Fig. 7.7. For each training example, if the class label is the target positive class name, keep the example unchanged. If the class label is not the target positive class name, change the class label to an unused class name, such as "other", to indicate that the example does not belong to the target class. While preprocessing the training data set, we also need to calculate the frequency of the target positive class. The frequency is used to choose the option of the training command of the SLIPPER rule learning system. We choose the option to make sure that the positive class is our target positive class for each binary classifier. The training data set could be quite large, for instance, the KDDCup'99 entire training data set contains about five millions examples, and its uncompressed file size is 743 M. The algorithm shown in Fig. 7.7 is optimized to reduce disk read.

As long as we get the right training data set for each target positive class, we can train the binary classifier for this class. Due to the dramatically varied distribution of training examples among all classes as well as subclasses, we did not use all 10% training data set of KDDCup'99 to train binary classifier for each class. Based on the distribution of each class, we use three different sets to train. When train binary classifier for class "DOS", we use all of the examples in the training data. When training binary classifiers for other classes, including "Normal", "PROBE", "R2L", and "U2R", we only keep up to the first 2,000 examples for each subclass of class "DOS". When training binary classifier for class "PROBE", "R2L", and "U2R", again, we remove most of the examples of class "Normal" from the training data set. Because there is no subclass for class "Normal", we keep first 3,000 examples of class "normal" to train binary classifiers for class "PROBE", "U2R", and "R2L".

After finishing training binary classifier for each class, we apply the binary classifier on its training data set to get the maximal prediction confidence for each classifier to compute the confidence ratio as well as the training data for our BP network. We use a tool called JavaNNS to train our BP neural networks. This software can be downloaded from http://www-ra.informatik.uni-tuebingen.de/downloads/JavaNNS. We can monitor the learning progress through an error graph window.

In our training experiments, we find that it is not necessary for the final arbiter equipped BP network to have very low training error to classify all training examples correctly. In contrast, using the first two arbitral strategies, the hybrid detection model cannot classify all training examples correctly. There are four misclassified training examples when we choose final prediction by confidence. And there are three misclassified training examples when we choose final prediction by confidence ratio. Training progress of the BP network is controlled by the loop number and the training error. It will be stopped when the detection model can classify all data in the training data set to avoid the overfitting problem.

7.3.3. *The MC-SLIPPER system and test performance*

7.3.3.1. *Overall detection performance*

To demonstrate the performance of our hybrid detection model shown in Fig. 7.8 we developed a system called multi-class SLIPPER (MC-SLIPPER)

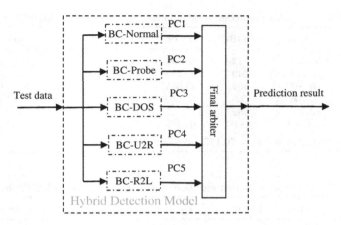

Fig. 7.8.   Hybrid detection model built from KDDCup'99 data set.

and applied MC-SLIPPER on KDDCup'99 intrusion detection test data set [84, 85]. To compare our experimental results with others' results, including the results of the KDDCup'99 competitions, we report our experimental results using confusion matrix, which is also used in KDDCup'99 contest. The main part of a confusion matrix has the same format with the misclassification cost matrix, but with different explanations for the entry: each entry CM (x, y) is the number of predictions whose predicted class is class y, but the actual class is class x. In order to compare the performance on different classes, we attach a column to the confusion matrix to list the accuracy of each class. In addition, one row of false-positive rate (FP-rate) for each class is added. Our results using three final prediction strategies (by Prediction Confidence (PC), by Prediction Confidence Ratio (PCR), and by Back Propagation Neural Network (BPNN)) are shown in Tables 7.15–7.17, respectively.

Table 7.15.   Detailed prediction results on test data set of MC-SLIPPER by PC.

	Normal	PROBE	DOS	U2R	R2L	Accuracy (%)
Normal	58,495	1,636	77	18	367	96.54
PROBE	293	3,600	183	1	89	86.41
DOS	5,554	902	223,074	16	307	97.05
U2R	113	66	0	33	16	14.47
R2L	12,914	2,133	0	7	1,135	7.01
FP-rate	24.39%	56.82%	0.12%	56%	40.70%	

Total misclassification cost = 72,494, false-negative rate = 7.54%

Intrusion Detection: A Machine Learning Approach

Table 7.16. Detailed prediction results on test data set of MC-SLIPPER by PCR.

	Normal	PROBE	DOS	U2R	R2L	Accuracy (%)
Normal	59,211	512	77	22	771	97.72
PROBE	273	3,540	184	3	166	84.97
DOS	5,547	362	223,615	16	313	97.28
U2R	106	66	0	37	19	16.23
R2L	12,556	2,052	1	7	1,573	9.72
FP-rate	23.79%	45.81%	0.12%	59.78%	44.65%	

Total misclassification cost = 70,177, false, negative rate = 7.38%

Table 7.17. Detailed prediction results on test data set of MC-SLIPPER by BPNN.

	Normal	PROBE	DOS	U2R	R2L	Accuracy (%)
Normal	59,049	537	83	18	906	97.45
PROBE	260	3,557	118	3	228	85.38
DOS	5,504	361	223,665	65	258	97.31
U2R	106	63	3	28	28	12.28
R2L	12,076	2,069	2	7	2,035	12.57
FP-rate	23.31%	46.00%	0.09%	76.86%	41.10%	

Total misclassification cost = 68,490, false, negative rate = 7.17%

From Tables 7.15 and 7.16, we can see that we get better performance using the second prediction strategy than using the first one just as we expect in terms of total misclassification cost (TMC). For the accuracy and false-positive rate for each class, only the accuracy of class "PROBE" is a little bit lower but with lower false-positive ratio; and the false-positive rates of class "U2R" and "R2L" are a slight higher but with higher accuracy. We get better performance using BP network than the first two prediction strategies further (see Table 7.17). The accuracy of class "U2R" is a little bit lower and its false-positive ratio is high. However, the accuracy of class "R2L" is much improved.

Compared with those results shown in Tables 7.5–7.9, the results of our hybrid detection model with all final arbiters are better than what the contest winner got. When using confidence ratio and BP network as the final prediction arbiter, the system generates the better performance than that of all other systems had. Our hybrid detection model equipped 5-7-5 BP network generates the lowest total misclassification cost. However, when our hybrid detection model equipped BP network, not only the final arbitration cost more time, but also needed to avoid the overfitting problem on training BP network. Figure 7.9 shows this overfitting problem. When the training

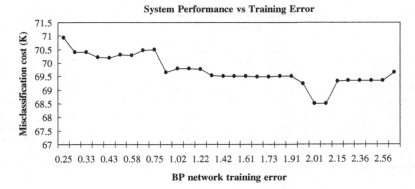

Fig. 7.9.   Overfitting of BP network.

error of the BP network was less than 2.01, if the training continued, although the training error was decreased, the overall detection performance (in terms of total misclassification cost) got worse. When a BP network will be trained on a new data set, try to stop the training process early to avoid the trained neural network overfit the training data. A helpful stop criterion is whether the detection model can classify all training data correctly.

7.3.3.2. *Detection capability on new attacks*

An intrusion detection system is going to be deployed to protect a real computer network system. A real computer network system is subjected to be attacked by new type of attacks, which will emerge very frequently. The detection capability on new attacks of an intrusion detection system is very important as well as the detection capability on known attacks. The KDDCup'99 intrusion detection data set can be used to evaluate this capability of a detection model in some degree, since 17 out of 38 types of attacks in the test data set are not presented in the training data set. A total of 18,729 out of 311,029 (about 6.0216%) examples in the test data set belong to these 17 new types attacks. Table 7.18 lists all new attacks in the test data set. Test results on new attacks of different systems are listed in Tables 7.19–7.21.

Data in Tables 7.19–7.21 were constructed from the data in Table 2 of the paper [88]. The test results of our MC-SLIPPER system built on hybrid detection model are shown in Tables 7.22 and 7.23, which has the lowest TMC and false-negative rate. Only the accuracy of "DOS" in our MC-SLIPPER system is a little bit lower than the accuracy of "DOS" in contest

Table 7.18.   New attacks in KDDCup'99 ID test data set.

Type/category	Count	Percentage (%)	Type/category	Count	Percentage (%)
mscan/PROBE	1,053	0.3386	apache2/DOS	794	0.2553
saint/PROBE	736	0.2366	mailbomb/DOS	5,000	1.6076
named/R2L	17	0.0055	processtable/DOS	759	0.2440
sendmail/R2L	17	0.0055	udpstorm/DOS	2	0.0006
snmpgetattack/R2L	7,741	2.4888	httptunnel/U2R	158	0.0508
snmpguess/R2L	2,406	0.7736	Ps/U2R	16	0.0051
worm/R2L	2	0.0006	sqlattack/U2R	2	0.0006
xlock/R2L	9	0.0029	xterm/U2R	13	0.0042
xsnoop/R2L	4	0.0013	ALL ATTACK	18,729	6.0216

Table 7.19.   Detailed prediction results on new attacks of contest winner.

	Normal	PROBE	DOS	U2R	R2L	Accuracy (%)
PROBE	511	1,097	181	0	0	61.32
DOS	5,297	1,024	234	0	0	3.57
U2R	153	20	0	12	4	6.35
R2L	10,188	5	0	3	0	0.00

Total misclassification cost = 53,766, false-negative rate = 86.22%

Table 7.20.   Detailed prediction results on new attacks of contest runner-up.

	Normal	PROBE	DOS	U2R	R2L	Accuracy (%)
PROBE	454	1,151	184	0	0	64.34
DOS	5,585	217	751	2	0	11.46
U2R	158	18	4	9	0	4.76
R2L	10,190	1	0	2	3	0.03

Total misclassification cost = 53,497, false-negative rate = 87.50%

Table 7.21.   Detailed prediction results on new attacks of PN-Rule.

	Normal	PROBE	DOS	U2R	R2L	Accuracy (%)
PROBE	864	693	23	3	206	38.74
DOS	6,423	33	0	99	0	0.00
U2R	173	2	0	6	8	3.17
R2L	10,192	0	0	4	0	0.00

Total misclassification cost = 55,720, false-negative rate = 94.25%

Table 7.22. Detailed prediction results on new attacks of MC-SLIPPER by PCR.

	Normal	PROBE	DOS	U2R	R2L	Accuracy (%)
PROBE	270	1,170	180	3	166	65.40
DOS	5,541	154	531	16	313	8.10
U2R	97	66	0	16	10	8.47
R2L	8,133	2,052	0	3	8	0.08

Total misclassification cost = 49,947, false-negative rate = 74.97%

Table 7.23. Detailed prediction results on new attacks of MC-SLIPPER by BPNN.

	Normal	PROBE	DOS	U2R	R2L	Accuracy (%)
PROBE	258	1,186	114	3	228	66.29
DOS	5,501	149	638	16	251	9.73
U2R	97	63	3	13	13	6.88
R2L	8,114	2,068	1	2	11	0.11

Total misclassification cost = 49,680, false-negative rate = 74.59%

runner-up (Tables 7.22 and 7.23). The test results show that our hybrid detection model is better to detect new attacks than other system does.

7.3.3.3. *Rule performance on final prediction*

The false prediction rate on test data set is an obvious parameter to evaluate the accuracy of rules. The count of final prediction that a rule contributes indicates how active a rule is. We collected those statistics from our experiment MC-SLIPPER by PCR on the test data set for each binary classifier as shown in Fig. 7.10. There were six rules (rule 1, 18, 21 in BC-Normal, rule 9 in BC-U2R, rule 1, 4 in BC-R2L) which didn't contribute to any final predictions on the test data set. However, some rules in BC-DOS contributed more than 100,000 final predictions. Figure 7.10 show that rules in each binary classifier have quite false rate, which varies from 0 to 100%. The statistics of rules with high false rate were summarized in Table 7.24. The row labeled "Rules Count" shows the number of rules that had the false rate indicated in the header. "ATP/Rule" means Average Total Predictions per rule and "AFP/Rule" is Average False Predictions per rule.

Since rules are learned by a boosting learning algorithm from training data set, which are expected to be roughly true. A rule with false rate over 0.4 is counted to rules with high false rates. However, these numbers of total or false predictions used in Table 7.24 are not the

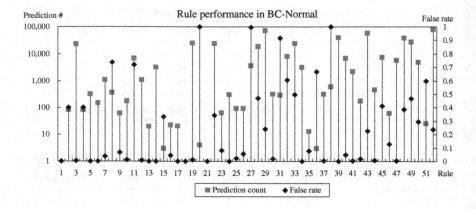

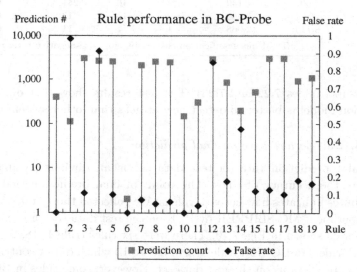

Fig. 7.10.   Rule performances on final predictions in our MC-SLIPPER.

sum of corresponding prediction number shown in Fig. 7.10, since usually multiple rules contribute to the same final prediction. The numbers used in Table 7.24 are weighted prediction counts. For example, if N rules contribute to a final prediction, only $1/N$ counts to each rule for this prediction. However, not all these N rules have same false rates. The numbers of total or false predictions are the sum of such weighted counts from each rule with certain high false rates.

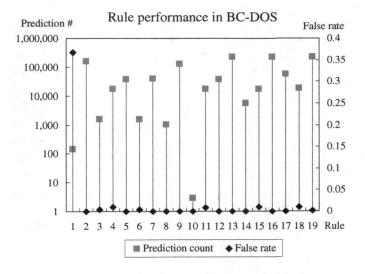

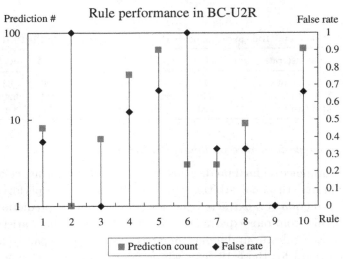

Fig. 7.10. (*Continued*)

The statistics shown in Table 7.24 are not satisfying. About 13% of the rules (15 out of 118) have false rates over 90% and these rules cover 1.1% of all predictions (3,435 out of 311,029); about 28% of the rules (33 out of 118) have false rate over 40% while covering 5.6% of all predictions.

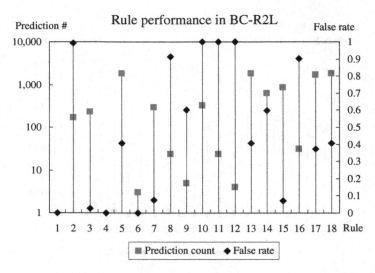

Fig. 7.10. (*Continued*)

Table 7.24. Rule performance with high false rate in MC-SLIPPER.

Rule false rate	=1	≥0.9	≥0.8	≥0.7	≥0.6	≥0.5	≥0.4
Rules count	7	15	15	17	25	26	33
ATP/Rule	41	229	229	273	254	244	529
AFP/Rule	41	223	223	252	218	209	326

7.3.3.4. *Rule performance on binary prediction*

Rule performance on final predictions depends on its performance on binary prediction and the final arbitral strategy. To assess rule performance on binary prediction, we extracted the sequence of binary prediction results for each rule from our experiments. Table 7.25 shows the statistical data for individual rules from different binary classifiers. For space reasons, we only show data for those 19 rules whose false prediction rates are greater than 20% and which cover more than 1% of all test data. These 19 rules contribute to 262,193 out of 299,471 false-positive predictions (87.55%) and have the biggest negative impact on the overall performance, when our hybrid detection model was tested on the KDDCup'99 test data set. In Table 7.25, the name of rule "xxxx_29" stands for the rule 29 in binary classifier "xxxx". The column titled "$P\#$" shows the false-positive binary predictions to which a rule contributes. Similarly, columns "$N\#$" and "$T\#$"

Table 7.25.   Selected rule performances on binary prediction in MC-SLIPPER.

Rule	$P\#$	$l=1$ (%)	$l=2$ (%)	$l \geq 3$ (%)	$l \geq 100$ (%)	$l \geq 1000$ (%)	$N\#$	$T\#$	FPR (%)
BC-Normal_29	17,335	21.80	10.55	67.66	31.22	22.43	8	53,862	24.36
BC-Normal_43	16,457	25.91	15.59	58.50	3.01	0.00	41	45,999	26.40
BC-PROBE_17	1,471	6.19	3.54	90.28	58.74	0.00	6	3,762	28.19
BC-PROBE_3	1,221	4.59	4.10	91.32	70.84	0.00	22	2,845	30.41
BC-Normal_50	2,384	13.76	7.30	78.94	22.73	0.00	46	4,143	36.97
BC-Normal_22	10,141	17.00	14.48	68.52	1.38	0.00	0	15,868	38.99
BC-Normal_48	15,497	16.64	11.74	71.61	17.22	0.00	13	23,965	39.29
BC-Normal_49	13,805	12.85	9.71	77.44	42.99	38.22	20	16,738	45.23
BC-PROBE_4	10,909	10.63	8.78	80.58	34.11	0.00	0	12,218	47.17
BC-Normal_28	9,179	7.31	6.69	86.00	6.58	0.00	2	10,072	47.69
BC-Normal_33	12,280	10.04	9.90	80.06	2.96	0.00	1	12,223	50.12
BC-Normal_45	5,018	2.21	1.95	95.83	38.36	0.00	6	4,313	53.81
BC-Normal_32	4,824	0.15	0.00	99.85	99.85	99.85	3	3,164	60.41
BC-Normal_11	4,875	0.04	0.00	99.96	99.96	99.96	0	1,894	72.02
BC-PROBE_12	11,109	1.52	1.73	96.75	59.84	0.00	0	2,787	79.94
BC-PROBE_16	40,917	0.08	0.04	99.88	99.19	87.17	108	3,032	93.12
BC-PROBE_5	40,519	0.06	0.03	99.91	99.53	94.86	0	2,368	94.48
BC-PROBE_7	40,705	0.02	0.00	99.97	99.90	99.19	0	2,117	95.06
BC-Normal_27	3,647	0.05	0.11	99.84	96.22	69.07	0	22	99.40

show the false-negative binary predictions and true binary predictions, respectively, for each rule. As can be seen from this table, the number of false-negative binary predictions is small compared to the number of false-positive binary predictions. The last column titled "FPR" is the overall false prediction rate, computed by $(P\# + N\#)/(P\# + N\# + T\#)$. l in the column titles refers to the number of successive false-positive predictions. When l is equal to 1, this false prediction is an isolated false prediction. We particularly examine the situations where long sequences of false-positive predictions occur.

7.3.4. *The ATIDS system and test performance*

The model tuning is triggered by the feedback from the last false prediction, and the updated model will be used to make predictions on new data. The tuning algorithm only solves how to tune the detection model after receiving the feedback on a false prediction from the system operator. However, it depends on the system operator whether the feedback on a false prediction is fed back to the model tuner and how long the feedback is delayed. Tuning triggered by isolated false prediction most likely will be a negative tuning. Property 3 also declares the possible risk when tuning is delayed too long. In the following, we examine the performance of our model tuning algorithm on the test data set with respect to how frequently and how soon tuning is performed. The test system is called automatically tuning IDS (ATIDS), and the block diagram of the test system is shown below. We put the system operator in the block diagram to show the interaction between the system and the operator (Fig. 7.11).

7.3.4.1. *Full and instant tuning*

In our first experiment, we assume that the user has enough time to verify the result of every prediction and every false prediction is identified and fed back to the model tuner. Before the system makes a prediction on the next data record, the model will be tuned instantly. The behavior of the system and its operator are summarized in pseudo code notation in Fig. 7.12. In practice, prediction and verification can occur simultaneously, as long as new data are not covered by a rule being verified.

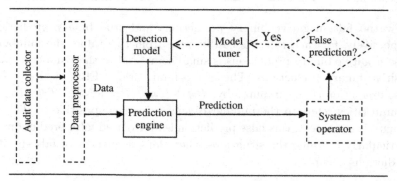

Fig. 7.11.   Block diagram of automatically tuning intrusion detection system (ATIDS).

```
LOOP
     INPUT Testdata (InputData):
     FinalResult = Predict (InputData);
     Feedback = Verify_Predition (InputData, FinalResult);
        IF ( is_false_ prediction (Feedback) Tune_Model (Feedback, FinalResult);
END
```

Fig. 7.12.   Pseudo code for full and instant tuning.

As long as tuning due to a false prediction by a rule is performed before new data covered by that rule is considered, tuning behaves as if instantaneously, although there is some delay.

We evaluated our tuning algorithm with full and instant tuning on the KDDCup'99 test data set. The results of tuned model with full and instant tuning when compared with the original hybrid detection model are shown in Table 7.26.

Compared with the results using original hybrid detection model, the total misclassification costs using tuned model drop roughly to 35% and the overall accuracy increases between 2.3% and 3.5%. Table 7.27 summarizes the rule performance on binary predictions for ATIDS and MC-SLIPPER.

The full and instant tuning are effective by taking advantage of Property 1. Especially for binary classifiers "BC-PROBE" and "BC-R2L", almost one-third of the rules in original model have over 50% false rates and more than two-thirds of the rules have over 20% false rates. But in tuned model, none of the rules has false rates over 20%. For binary classifier "BC-Normal", only one rule has over 50% false rate. Three other rules have over 20% false rates. The false rate with respect to binary prediction

Table 7.26.   Performance of tuned model with full and instant tuning.

Final arbiter	Test system	Overall accuracy (%)	TMC	(%) TMC
BP network	ATIDS	95.06	45,002	65.70
	MC-SLIPPER	92.70	68,490	
Confidence ratio	ATIDS	95.52	46,096	65.68
	MC-SLIPPER	92.59	70,177	
Confidence	ATIDS	95.53	47,306	65.25
	MC-SLIPPER	92.06	72,494	

Table 7.27.   Comparison of rule performance on binary predictions.

Binary classifier	Total number of rules	Number of rules with false rate >50%		Number of rules with false rate >20%	
		ATIDS	MC-SLIPPER	ATIDS	MC-SLIPPER
BC-Normal	52	1	9	4	24
BC-PROBE	19	0	6	0	14
BC-DOS	19	0	0	1	1
BC-U2R	10	1	1	3	3
BC-R2L	18	0	6	0	13

for rule 29 in binary classifier "BC-Normal" drops from 24.34% to 6.64%. However, we notice that four rules exhibit worse performance after the tuning procedure. Rule 16 in binary classifier "BC-Normal" covers 22 data records and the false rate increases from 4.55% to 9.09%. Rule 25 in binary classifier "BC-Normal" covers 123 data records and the false rate increases from 5.69% to 12.20%. Rule 36 in binary classifier "BC-Normal" covers three data records and the false rate increases from 33.33% to 66.67%. Rule 9 in binary classifier "BC-U2R" covers 62 data records and the false rate increases from 24.19% to 29.03%. We analyzed the predictions on the data records covered by those four rules and found that Property 3 could be used to explain the degraded performance of rules 16 and 25 in binary classifier "BC-Normal". In the predictions made by original detection model, the sole false prediction on the data covered by rule 16 is an isolated false prediction and all the seven false predictions on the data covered by rule 25 are isolated false predictions. After tuning on rules 16 and 25, the tuned model makes a new false prediction on the next data record covered by rules 16 and 25, respectively, while the original model predicted correctly. For rule 36 in binary classifier "BC-Normal", the tuned model makes a false prediction on the first data record covered by rule 36 and the other three rules discussed, while the original detection makes true prediction on that data record. The reason here is that the other three rules were tuned before they encountered this data record.

The full and instant tuning is effective in improving system performance, but certainly not perfect. In any case, in practice it is almost impossible for the user to verify every prediction due to the huge amount of data the system processes. In the next subsection, we will examine how the tuning algorithm performs when only partial of false prediction could be used to tune the detection model.

7.3.4.2. *Partial but instant tuning*

In the next experiment, the detection model will again be tuned instantaneously, but only some false predictions are fed back to tune the model. For example, if only 20% of the false predictions can be caught in time and their corrections fed back into the detection model, will model tuning provide any benefit? The pseudo code for partial tuning is shown in Fig. 7.13. All predictions are verified, but only some of the false predictions are used to tune the model. All other false predictions are ignored, simulating false predictions which are not caught (Table 7.30).

```
LOOP
    INPUT Testdata (InputData):
    FinalResult = Predict (InputData);
    Feedback = Verify_Predition (InputData, FinalResult);
    IF ( is_false_ prediction (Feedback) AND should_tune_model () )
        Tune_Model (Feedback, FinalResult);
END
```

Fig. 7.13.   Pseudo code for partial and instant tuning.

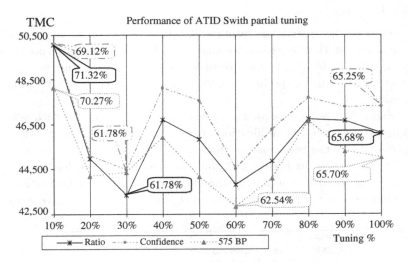

Fig. 7.14.   Performances of ATIDS with partial tuning.

In this experiment, we control the percentage of false predictions used to tune the model. We performed a set of experiments, letting the portion of false predictions used to tune the model ranging from 10% to 100%. The results are shown in Fig. 7.14.

The labels show the ratio of TMC, comparing tuned detection model with original model. The total misclassification costs of detection model with 10% partial tuning drops about 30% compared to original model. The detection model is tuned with feedback from the last false prediction. Whether the tuning will yield more accurate predictions depends on the subsequent covered data. If the model is tuned according to a false prediction on which is at the beginning of a false prediction cluster (made by the original detection model), then the tuning could reduce many false predictions. But if the model is tuned on an isolated false prediction, the tuned model might make a new false prediction on the next covered data where the original model made a true prediction. The extreme examples are the four rules discussed at the end of the previous subsection, which have worse performance after tuning. With partial tuning, some isolated false predictions might be skipped to tune the model, which could reduce the new false predictions made by the tuned model. So a higher tuning percentage does not guarantee a lower TMC, as clearly visible in Fig. 7.14.

7.3.4.3. *Delayed tuning*

In practice, the system operators will take some time to verify a false prediction, yet the positive rules that contributed to the false prediction might cover subsequent data records. Consequentially, tuning will be delayed. In a third experiment, detection model with delayed tuning is examined.

Figure 7.15 shows the pseudo code for the detection model with delayed tuning. Prediction and verification are now independent of each other (as represented by the two separate threads in Figure 7.15, and delay may be incurred between prediction and the consideration of the feedback from verification. In the experiment, the verification thread is simulating the system operator verifying the predictions, and the delay can be controlled

```
LOOP
    INPUT Testdata (InputData):
        FinalResult = Predict_Data (Data);
        SEND PredictionResult (Data, FinalResult);
    INPUT Feedback (Feedback, Data):
        Tune_Model (Data);
END
```

a. Pseudo code for prediction thread

```
LOOP
    INPUT PredictionResult (InputData);
    Feedback = Verify_Predition (Data);
    IF ( is_false_prediction (Feedback) )
        SEND Feedback (Feedback, Data);
END
```

b. Pseudo code for verification thread

Fig. 7.15.   Pseudo code for delayed tuning.

Table 7.28. Performance of ATIDS with delayed tuning.

Test system	Tuning delayed seconds	Overall accuracy (%)	TMC	TMC (%)
MC-SLIPPER		92.59	70,177	
ATIDS	1–3	94.61	55,982	79.77
ATIDS	4–10	94.30	54,841	78.15
ATIDS	10–20	90.30	80,186	114.26
ATIDS	4–20	94.49	56,087	79.97

randomly within certain limitation. Since the data in test data set don't include any timing information. In our experiments with delayed tuning, a preprocessing thread sent test data to prediction thread one by one every 40–80 milliseconds to simulate the network traffic flow.

The results of the detection model with delayed tuning are shown in Table 7.28. The experimental results show that the performance depends on the delayed time. When tuning is not delayed too long, the impact of tuning is positive, and the system gains performance improvement from tuning. But when tuning is delayed to long, the overall impact of tuning is negative, as demonstrated by the experiment with 10–20 seconds delay. Property 3 stated that the false rate of a rule might change dramatically even in adjoining segments. In this experiment, it will take 20–40 seconds to predict the 500 records in one segment. If tuning is delayed 20 seconds in a segment with high false prediction rate, after tuning is complete, the system might predict on the data record in the next segment. If the original false prediction rate in the second segment is low, the updated model could then make many false predictions. A small delay in tuning, however, has positive impact on system performance. In the experiment with 4–20 seconds delay, 129 false predictions are used to tune the model and 71 instances feedback are delayed more than 10 seconds as shown in Fig. 7.16, yet still has lower TMC (Tables 7.29 and 7.30). Some negative tuning could be avoided: If it takes too much time to identify a false prediction, the tuning on this false prediction could be skipped as long as the prediction result is not fed back to the model tuner.

The 1–3 seconds, 4–10 seconds, 10–20 seconds, and 4–20 seconds delays reported in Table 7.28 refer to the actual time taken in our experiments. Remember that the test data were constructed from the network traffic of two weeks, which yielded around two million connection records. 4–20 seconds delay in our experiments is equivalent to 0.5–3 minutes delay in real time.

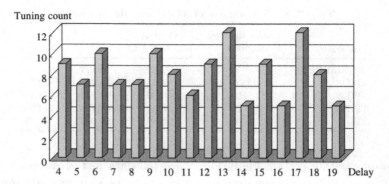

Fig. 7.16.   Statistics of tuning count on delayed seconds in ATIDS.

Table 7.29.   Detailed prediction results on test data set of ATIDS with delay tuning.

	Normal	PROBE	DOS	U2R	R2L	Accuracy (%)
Normal	59,644	441	345	28	135	98.43
PROBE	146	3,680	170	28	142	88.33
DOS	2,789	206	226,721	2	135	98.64
U2R	44	38	96	41	9	17.98
R2L	11,275	85	1,015	14	3,800	23.47
FP-rate	19.29%	17.30%	0.71%	63.72%	9.97%	

Total misclassification cost = 56,087, false-negative rate = 6.69%

Table 7.30.   Detailed prediction results on new attacks of ATIDS with delay tuning.

	Normal	PROBE	DOS	U2R	R2L	Accuracy (%)
PROBE	144	1,323	152	28	142	73.95
DOS	2,772	118	3,535	2	128	53.93
U2R	35	38	94	18	4	9.52
R2L	9,527	82	574	4	9	0.09

Total misclassification cost = 46,515, false-negative rate = 66.62%

To compare rule performance on final predictions, we collected the data from the experiment for tuning delay 4–20 seconds while employing the prediction confidence ratio based on the final arbitral strategy. The statistics of rule performance with high false rate are shown in Table 7.31.

Compared with statistics shown in Table 7.24, although the total number of rules with high false rate has not improved considerably (28–33), the average number of total predictions made by one of those rules with

Table 7.31. Rule performance with high false rate in ATIDS.

Rule false rate	=1	≥0.9	≥0.8	≥0.7	≥0.6	≥0.5	≥0.4
Rules count	8	10	14	17	20	24	28
ATP/rule	33	48	49	56	80	130	246
AFP/rule	33	48	47	50	63	86	132

high false rate has dropped to 46.4% (246–529) and the average number of false predictions made by one of those rules with high false rate dropped to 40.6% (132–326).

In delayed tuning, the user burden is quite low since the percentage of false predictions used to tune the model is low. For example, in the experiment with 4–10 seconds delay, only 230 false predictions are used to tune the model, which is only 1.3% of all false predictions. In our experiment with 4–20 seconds delay, 129 false predictions were used to tune the model, which is only 0.75% of all false predictions.

7.3.5. *The ADAT IDS system and test performance*

The system architecture for ADAT IDS in our experiments is shown in Fig. 6.1. The final arbiter in hybrid detection model adopts the prediction confidence ratio-based strategy. The preprocessing thread still sent test data to prediction thread one by one every 40–80 milliseconds. And the verification costs 4–20 seconds. Since suspicious predictions are buffered in the prediction queue. They take some time in the queue to wait for the verification. So the feedback on the false prediction will be delayed more seconds.

7.3.5.1. *Detection performance*

We ran 20 times of our experiments, and the total misclassification cost (TMC) for each run is shown in Fig. 7.17. The average TMC of these 20 runs is 52,401 and the standard deviation is 2,972. Table 7.32 is the detailed prediction results of experiment running. No. 4, which shows our ADAT IDS could improve the overall accuracy while decreasing the total misclassification cost. The ADAT IDS reduced about 25.5% total misclassification cost, while increasing about 1.78% overall accuracy compared to the MC-SLIPPER system (see the result in Table 7.16). Compared to the results of ATIDS with delayed tuning (delay 4–20 seconds) shown in Table 7.28, although the overall accuracy is a little bit lower, the TMC increased 6.8% (Table 7.33).

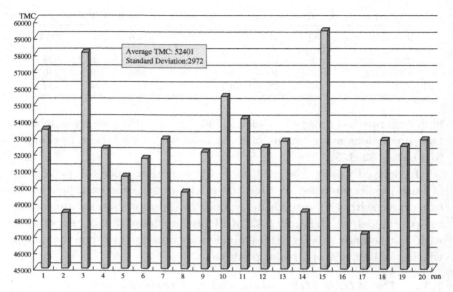

Fig. 7.17. A set of experimental results of our ADAT IDS.

Table 7.32. Detailed prediction results on test data set of ADAT IDS.

	Normal	PROBE	DOS	U2R	R2L	Accuracy (%)
Normal	57,751	257	1,832	54	699	95.31
PROBE	125	3,680	218	10	133	88.33
DOS	900	201	228,092	156	504	99.23
U2R	39	37	100	30	22	13.16
R2L	8,897	78	3,234	26	3,954	24.42
FP-rate	14.71%	13.47%	2.31%	89.13%	25.56%	

Total misclassification cost = 52,294, overall accuracy = 94.37%

7.3.5.2. *Rule performance on final prediction*

Table 7.34 exhibits the statistic of rule performance on final prediction of our ADAT IDS. Although the counts of rules with high false rate in ADAT IDS are comparable with the corresponding count shown in Tables 7.24 and 7.28, the prediction counts drop dramatically. The average number of predictions made by one of those rules with high false rate over 40% in ADAT IDS has dropped to 14.6% (77–529) of the average number of predictions made by one of those rules with high false rate over 40% in MC-SLIPPER and 31.5% (77–246) of the average number of predictions made by one of those rules with high false rate over 40% in ATIDS. The

Table 7.33. Detailed prediction results on new attack of ADAT IDS.

	Normal	PROBE	DOS	U2R	R2L	Accuracy (%)
PROBE	124	1,341	181	10	133	74.96
DOS	898	150	4,855	156	496	74.07
U2R	31	37	96	11	14	5.82
R2L	8,578	76	1,528	4	10	0.10

Total misclassification cost = 41,937, false-negative rate = 51.42%

Table 7.34. Rule performance with high false rate in ADAT IDS.

Rule false rate	=1.0	≥0.9	≥0.8	≥0.7	≥0.6	≥0.5	≥0.4
Rules count	8	14	16	17	19	22	26
TP/rule	45	52	51	49	48	48	77
FP/rule	45	52	50	47	45	42	53

average number of false predictions made by one of those rules with high false rate over 40% in ADAT IDS had dropped to 16.3% (53–326) of the average number of false predictions made by one of the rules with high false rate over 40% in MC-SLIPPER and to 40.1% (53–132) of the average number of weighted false predictions made by rules with high false rate over 40% in ATIDS.

A total of 68 rules in ADAT IDS were tuned while the system was running. A total of 23 rules among these 68 rules have high false rate over 40% in MC-SLIPPER, and 18 rules among these 68 rules have over 40% false rate in ATIDS, while only 14 rules among these 68 rules have over 40% false rate in ADAT IDS as shown in Table 7.35. Tunings on those 68 rules

Table 7.35. Comparison of rule performance of 68 tuned rules in ADAT IDS.

Rule false rate	MC-SLIPPER			ATIDS			ADAT		
	Rules count	TP/ rule	FP/ rule	Rules count	TP/ rule	FP/ rule	Rules count	TP/ rule	FP/ rule
=1	2	60	60	2	28	28	3	7	7
≥0.9	8	390	378	4	68	67	7	39	37
≥0.8	8	390	378	7	68	64	9	40	38
≥0.7	10	431	397	10	74	64	10	37	34
≥0.6	18	334	284	13	108	81	12	38	34
≥0.5	18	334	284	16	181	115	13	44	36
≥0.4	23	723	444	18	367	193	14	106	64

Table 7.36.   Statistics on predictions passed fuzzy prediction filter.

	Normal	PROBE	DOS	U2R	R2L
Normal	168	15	6	1	5
PROBE	5	15	1	0	1
DOS	5	4	15	0	1
U2R	5	6	0	3	0
R2L	33	7	3	2	3

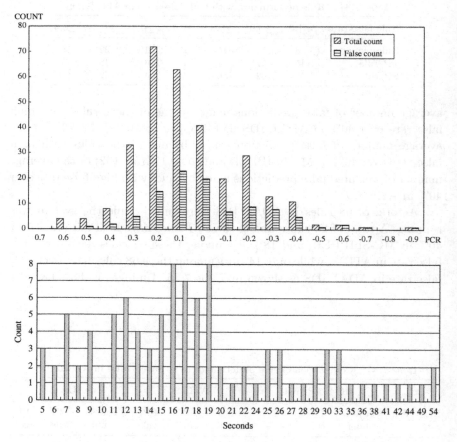

Fig. 7.18.   Statistic of tuning count on delayed seconds in ADAT IDS.

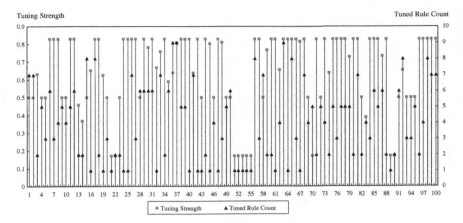

Fig. 7.19.   Tuning strength and tuned rule count for all 100 tunes.

in ADAT IDS drop the average number of false prediction per rule to 14.4% of the average number of total predictions per rule made by one of those rules with high false rate in MC-SLIPPER and to reduce about 33.2% the average number of false predictions made by those rules in ATIDS.

7.3.5.3. *Performance of prediction filter*

The burden on the user was light, and only 304 suspect predictions passed through the fuzzy prediction filter, where 100 predictions were verified to be false (Table 7.36).

The statistics of tuning count on delayed feedback are shown in Fig. 7.18.

The tuning strengths varied from about 0.17–0.83. The tuning strengths and the count of tuned rule of all 100 tunes are shown in Fig. 7.19.

Part B

Intrusion Detection for Wireless Sensor Network

In this part, we focus on the intrusion detection problem in wireless sensor network.

Chapter 8

Attacks against Wireless Sensor Network

8.1. Wireless Sensor Network

A wireless sensor network (WSN) consists of a large set of tiny sensor nodes. Sensor nodes can perform sensing, data processing, and communicating but with limited power, computational capacities, small memory size, and low bandwidth [42]. The sensor nodes in WSNs are usually static after deployment, and communicate mainly through broadcast instead of point-to-point communication. Sensor networks have been used in a variety of domains, such as military sensing in battlefield, perimeter defense on critical area such as airport, intrusion detection for traditional communication network, disasters monitoring, home healthcare, and so on. Obviously, some applications are security critical, which attract many researchers' attention to secure a sensor network. Some security protocols or mechanisms have been designed for sensor network. For example, SPINS, a set of protocols, provides secure data confidentiality, two-party data authentication, and data freshness and authenticated broadcast for sensor network [91]. LEAP, a localized encryption and authentication protocol, is designed to support in-network processing based on the different security requirements for different types of messages exchange [92]. INSENS is an intrusion tolerant routing protocol for wireless sensor networks [93]. A lightweight security protocol relying solely on broadcasts of end-to-end encrypted packets was reported in [94]. However, a sensor network, as a complicated system, there are always some vulnerabilities to be attacked. In this part, we will investigate intrusion detection approach in sensor network and its related topics.

8.2. Challenges on Intrusion Detection in WSNs

Security properties or the challenges of the wireless sensor networks have been report in varied literatures [42, 95–97]. We summarized the challenges on designing IDS in WSN from the limited resources of the sensor nodes, the wireless communication, the dynamic topology of the network, and the hostile working environment [98].

Sensor network nodes usually have severely constraint in computational power, memory size, and energy. A representative processor used in well-known Crossbow MICA2/MICAz series sensor nodes is an 8-MHz 8-bit Atmel ATMEGA128L CPU. This CPU has only 128 kB of instruction memory, 4 kB of RAM for data, and 512 kB of flash memory [99]. The sensor node power is usually provided by 2 AA batteries. With those limited resources, some effective security defense techniques for traditional LAN/WAN/Internet are no longer suitable for wireless sensor network. For example, asymmetric cryptography is often too expensive for many WSN applications. Intrusion detection, as another layer of security, plays a more important role to secure wireless sensor networks. However, the low computational power and the insufficient available memory pose big challenges to the design of an intrusion detection system for WSN: the intrusion detection components should optimize resource consumption, and it might sacrifice its performance to fit the resource constraints. Another challenge is the available data, due to low available storage (if it has), only limited log/audit data could be used for intrusion detection.

Sensor nodes use wireless communication in WSNs. Any information over the radio can be intercepted and the private or sensitive information could be captured by a passive attacker. An aggressive attacker can easily inject malicious messages into the wireless network to perform varied attacks. Unlike wireless local area networks (LANs), whose available bandwidths could be 54 Mbps, the data rate for WSN is likely far less than 1 Mbps. For example, the Crossbow MICA2 series motes feature a multichannel radio from Chipcon, delivering up to 38.4 kbps data rate with a range of up to 1,000 feet [100]. The MICAz series motes offer 250 Kpbs data rate with a range of up to 100 m [101]. The low bandwidth prevents some analysis on suspicious data being executed promptly in the powerful remote base station. On the other hand, communication is a very energy-hungry task in sensor node, transmitting with maximal power could consume about 3–4 times power as processor does in active mode. Most of communication ability should be reserved for target-sensed information.

Only limited amount of security-related data could be sent to powerful base station for further comprehensive analysis to detect intrusions.

Knowledge of the network is a very useful information to detect intrusions. In a wireless sensor network, the topology of the network is usually not *a priori*. Even after the deployment, the network is always evolving due to frequent failure of sensor nodes, new added sensor nodes. It could be a big challenge to build a base profile in such a dynamic network for an intrusion detection system.

WSNs may be deployed in hostile environments such as battlefields, where sensor nodes are susceptible to physical capture. Security information (e.g., shared key) might be exposed by compromised nodes. The development of tamper-proof nodes is one possible approach to security in hostile environment, but the complicated hardware and high cost keep it away from WSN applications. An intrusion detection system for WSN has to handle physical attacks as well as network attacks.

8.3. Attacks against WSNs

Researchers have identified some of attacks that could be performed against wireless sensor networks. In this section, we will discuss those attacks. One of the most challenging issues that sensor networks face is how to resist against physical attacks. In traditional computer communication network, physical security is often taken for granted. Attackers are simply denied physical access to network nodes. Since wireless sensor networks might be deployed in hostile environment or densely populated areas, it is very hard to prevent sensor nodes from being accessed and captured physically. A captured sensor could be simply disabled to destruct the network. Or the memory in the captured sensor node could be analyzed to expose its data or cryptographic keys. The exposed key could be used to perform further attacks. A captured sensor node could be reprogrammed by the attacker and be re-joined to the network in the form of a subverted sensor node [96], which is potentially undetectable to neighboring nodes.

Jamming is a well-known, denial-of-service attack on wireless communication. Different layers could be targeted by jamming attack. At the physical layer, the attacker can send out interfering RF signals to impede communication. The jamming attacker can also inject irrelevant data to waste/drain battery energy on the receiving node for radio reception. Link-layer jamming exploits properties of the medium access control protocol employed. For instance, the attack can induce malicious collisions or attempt to get an unfair share of the radio resource [102]. At network/routing layer, an attacker injects malicious routing information that causes other nodes to form a routing loop to waste precious communication and battery resources.

Misdirection is an attack against routing algorithms that can be performed by spoofed, altered, replayed routing information. By forwarding messages along wrong paths, an attacker misdirects them, perhaps by advertising false routing updates [102]. An attacker could inflict the attack on a particular sender by diverting only traffic originating from the victim node.

A sinkhole attack is also against the routing algorithms in a WSN. It typically works by making a compromised node to allure nearly all the traffic from a particular area through the node, forming a routing hole [103]. Through a sinkhole attack, the compromised node on the path that packets follow can enable many other attacks, like selective forwarding.

In a selective forwarding attack, the compromised nodes simply drop certain messages to ensure that those messages are not forwarded any further, but forward the other traffic as normal to reduce the risk being detected [103]. An extreme form of selective forwarding attack, called black hole attack [102], is that a malicious node refuses to forward every packet. However, such black hole attack runs the risk of its neighboring nodes concluding that the malicious has failed and decided to seek another route.

The Sybil attack is where a malicious node illegitimately claims multiple identities and works as if it were many nodes [104]. The identities could be stolen or fabricated. The Sybil attack can be exploited at different layers to cause denial-of-service in sensor networks [102]. At the MAC layer, the malicious node can claim a dominating fraction of the shared radio resource by Sybil attack. At the routing layer, by claiming a large number of identities, the Sybil node (the node performing Sybil attack) will be selected as the next hop node with high probability to create a "sinkhole". Any system whose correct behavior is based on the assumption that most nodes will behave properly may be at the risk for Sybil attacks. For example, in WSN, usually aggregation of sensor readings rather than individual sensor reading will be sent to base station to conserve energy. By using the Sybil attack, one malicious node may be able to contribute to the aggregate many times to alter the aggregate reading.

In the wormhole attack, an adversary tunnels messages received in one part of the network over a low latency link and replays them in a different part [105]. The simplest instance of this attack is a single node situated between two other nodes forwarding messages between the two of them. However, wormhole attacks will more commonly involve two distant malicious nodes colluding to understate their distance from each other by relaying packets along an out-of-bound channel available only to the attacker.

HELLO flooding attack is against many node discovery protocols. Those protocols require nodes to broadcast HELLO packets to announce their existences to their neighbors, and a node receiving such a packet may recognize the sender as its neighbor according to the normal radio range. This assumption could be attacked by using a laptop-class node which can broadcast HELLO packets with large enough transmission power that could convince every node in the network that the adversary was its neighbor [103].

Rushing attack is against many flooding-based broadcast algorithms, which employ duplicate suppression on incoming messages where a node only forwards a message once and drops the duplicate message with the same ID. All nodes under the rushing attack will suppress the legitimate broadcast message if a bogus message with the same message ID has been broadcast by an attacker [106].

A stealthy attack is to deliberately deceive the network with a false data value [107]. This attack is mainly against the data aggregation scenario. There are several methods to alter the normal aggregation result. For instance, a compromised sensor/aggregator can report significantly biased false values. A compromised node can also perform a Sybil attack to have greater impact on the aggregated result. The attacker can also perform denial-of-service attacks on legitimate nodes to suppress their impact on the aggregation result. A stealthy attack can also be executed to disseminate false timing information to desynchronize nodes in the network by intercepting and delaying synchronization messages, or spreading false synchronization messages [96].

Chapter 9

Intrusion Detection System for Wireless Sensor Network

9.1. Architecture of IDS for WSN

For the traditional wired network, four architectures of intrusion detection system were studied. Centralized network intrusion detection systems are characterized by distributed audit collection and centralized analysis. A hierarchical NIDS has some intermediate components between the collection and analysis components to form a tree structure hierarchy. The intermediate components aggregate, abstract, and reduce the collected data and output the results to analysis. A netted architecture permits information flow from any node to any other node. The collection, aggregation, and analysis components are combined into a single component that is residing on every monitored system. In a mobile agent-based intrusion detection system, all of collection, aggregation, and analysis components are wrapped by mobile agent. The code can be migrated to a destination instead of passing massive audit data to reduce the network traffic. Although a centralized detection algorithm was proposed to detect *sinkhole/selective forwarding* attack in wireless sensor network in [108]. However, the centralized architecture is not suitable for an intrusion detection system to detect as many types of attacks as possible, because the low data rate of wireless communication and limited energy of the sensor nodes couldn't afford to pass the massive audit data to base station to be analyzed. On other hand, the codes in the sensor nodes are written in its ROM before the sensor network is deployed. There is no feasible solution to support accepting and executing code dynamically which is

147

required by the mobile agent-based architecture. A hierarchical architecture of IDS was suggested in [109], where the local agent monitors the node local activity to detect intrusions and the global agent monitors the packets sent by its all neighbors to detect attacks. The local agents run on every sensor nodes while the global agents run on selected nodes, such as the cluster head in applications deploying hierarchical routing protocols, or some watchdog nodes. A decentralized high-level rule-based IDS model was proposed in [100]. Like in the netted architecture, all IDS functions, from data acquiescing to analyzing, are implemented in monitor nodes. However, unlike in the netted architecture, only selected sensor nodes act as monitor nodes and only intrusion alerts are sent to base station.

In our intrusion detection system, the architecture is similar with the netted architecture, where every sensor node will be equipped an intrusion detection agent (IDA) [118]. But no cooperation exists between two IDAs since no node can be trusted. Like the attacks against the traditional wired network, the attacks in wireless sensor network could be inside attacks or outside attacks. The outside attacks could come from more powerful adversary nodes like laptop, while the inside attacks might be launched by compromised sensor nodes that have the legitimate access to the sensor network. Sensor networks are application-oriented, the codes in the sensor nodes are written in its ROM before the sensor network is deployed. An adversary can physically capture a sensor node from a sensor network and reprogram it with extracted security sensitive data (such as id, key) and malicious codes. The subverted node could join the senor network to attack the sensor network further as a compromised node. Unlike the traditional wired network, where Host-based Intrusion Detection System (HIDS) can analyze the host features to detect whether the host is compromised or misused. We cannot expect to design a similar intrusion detection component to report that its host node is compromised or misused because all original codes (including intrusion detection codes) in its ROM could be erased or modified in such a compromised node. However, we could design a similar Local Intrusion Detection Component (LIDC) to analyze local features to detect whether its host node is suffering attack by other malicious nodes.

One of the goals of intrusion detection is to stop any ongoing attacks if it is possible. Wireless sensor networks mainly rely on wireless broadcast communication with certain effective range, thus it is possible to locate the inside intruder (subverted node) and isolate it from the sensor network. To locate the subverted node, the intrusion detection system must

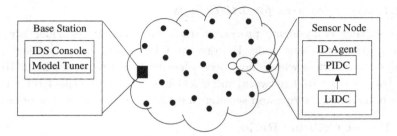

Fig. 9.1. An intrusion detection system for wireless sensor network.

monitor some suspect nodes and identify subverted nodes by monitoring communication activities of neighbor nodes, which is the task of Packet-based Intrusion Detection Component (PIDC) in our IDS. However, the density of nodes in wireless sensor networks is usually high. Many WSN-related research works were based on the network where each node had eight or more neighbor nodes. If a PIDC has to monitor communication activities of its all neighbor nodes, it will cost too much of its rare energy. Based on the analysis of the LIDC, the IPDC could monitor only one or couple of its neighbor nodes which could be particular suspect nodes. The PIDCs in its watchdog nodes could cooperate together to identify the real subverted node.

The intrusion alerts are sent to the base station, where the user may be able to verify some possible intrusion. For some false alerts, the base station could do some tuning of the intrusion detection model to reduce further false alerts, and pass the tuning result to sensor nodes. The system block diagram of our proposed intrusion detection is shown Fig. 9.1.

9.2. Audit Data in WSN

In the domain of intrusion detection for traditional wired network, comprehensive research works have been done on the audit data for intrusion detection. Many system features were identified to be useful for intrusion detection. For example, 41 features were conducted on the network connection in the KDDCup'99 Intrusion Detection data set. However, due to the resource constraints of a sensor node, there are only few features that could be used to detect intrusion. Moreover, a sensor network will have its own application requirement and employ only necessary protocols. Thus not all of features identified below could be available for one particular sensor network application.

9.2.1. *Local features for LIDC in WSN*

The sensing component, processor, radio and energy provider are the core parts of a sensor node. Besides the CPU usage, memory usage and changes on storage which have been identified to detect attacks in HIDS for traditional wired network, more features can be identified related on communication, energy, and sensing to detect intrusion in sensor node.

(a) **Packet Collision Ratio**

Packet collision occurs when two or more neighbor sensor nodes try to send packet at the same time through the shared communication channel. Collided packets have to been discarded and retransmitted and waste the constrained energy. Collisions are handled by MAC (Media Access Control) protocol. Scheduled protocols (such as TDMA-based LEACH [111]) are collision free protocols and all transmissions are scheduled on different time/frequency slots. However, adversary nodes could break the schedule intended to attack the sensor network. Contention-based protocols (such as CSMA-based protocol [112]) allocate the shared channel on-demand and employ some mechanism to avoid the collision but accept some level collisions. A good MAC protocol should archive relative low collision rate when the sensor network works normally, thus abnormal high collision ratio indicates the existence of adversary.

(b) **Packet Collision Ratio**

In contention-based MAC protocols, a packet will be buffered to wait for the shared channel. The fairness of accessing shared channel of the MAC protocol will ensure the waiting time of a packet in a reasonable level. The statistic of waiting time could be used to detect some attacks against the fairness of MAC protocol.

(c) **RTS Packets Rate**

To avoid packet collision, contention-based MAC protocols adopt RTS/CTS mechanism. When the channel is idle, the sender is required to send Request-to-Send (RTS) packet to the receiver, and the receiver acknowledges the Clear-to-Send (CTS) packet. The sender starts to send its data after receiving the CTS packet from the receiver. This RTS/CTS mechanism could be attacked by sending lots of RTS packets to gain unfair channel or to exhaust the receiver's energy.

(d) **Neighbor Count**

Sensor nodes have limited radio transmission range, while the sensor network could be very large. A large sensor network usually employs a multi-hop routing protocol to communication. Each sensor node maintains a neighbor table to record its neighbor information (e.g., nodes id, link cost, etc.) to build its routing. Unlike the mobile ad hoc network (MANET), most of nodes in sensor network are supposed to be stationary. The neighbor table should be stable in relative short period, although new nodes could be added and existed node could be removed since fault or energy exhaust over a long time. The change in its neighbor count could be used to detect some attacks. For example, the *Sybil attack* is where a malicious node illegitimately claims multiple identities and works as if it were many nodes.

(e) **Routing Cost**

In wireless sensor network, a multi-hop routing protocol maintains a route table in every node to route its packets. The route table mainly records the next node of the path from one node to base station and its cost, such as hop count or latency. Attacks against routing protocol (such as sinkhole/wormhole) usually broadcast fake routing information to attract more packets to route to its node. Monitoring the routing cost and analyzing its change could be used to detect those attacks.

(f) **Power Consumption Rate**

Sensor nodes have constrained power. The components of the sensor node, including processing unit, sensing unit, and radio, are designed to be powered off to save the energy if it is possible. The node spends most of time in sleep mode to extend the node life. Some proposed energy-aware routing protocols (e.g., SPIN) has access to the current energy level of the node and adapts the protocol it is running based on how much energy is remaining. Some DOS (Denial of Service) attacks aim at the limit power of the sensor nodes. For example, an intruder interfere the transmission to increase the collision ratio or send RTS packets flood to exhaust the victim's energy. The power consumption ratio could monitor to detect such attacks. Usually sensor node (e.g., MICA2/MICAz nodes) has its own resource manager which keeps track of resource consumption including the power consumption.

(g) **Sensing Reading Report Rate**

Sensing is one of the main functions of sensor nodes. Different applications have different sensing reading report requirements. Some applications require each sensor node report its reading periodically. In these applications, if a sensor node couldn't report its sensing reading following the desired interval, the sensing component could be under attacks. Some other applications require each sensor node report its reading as the answer of the query from the base station. Subverted node could query the sensing reading more frequently to exhaust the energy of victim nodes.

9.2.2. *Packet features for PIDC in WSN*

Packet-based Intrusion Detection Component (PIDC) analyzes the packets from a suspect node to know whether the suspect node is attacking the host node. The following identified features are calculated on the packets from the same sender (a suspect node).

(a) **Distribution of Packet Type**

There are several packets to be transmitted over the air in the wireless sensor network, such as sensing data, route update, query/command from the base station, and HELLO packets. But the main purpose of a sensor network is to sense certain interesting information, thus the main part of the packets should be sensing data.

(b) **Packet Received Signal Strength**

In wireless transmission, the sender radiates electromagnetic energy into the air through its antenna and the receiver picks up the electromagnetic wave from its surrounding air through its antenna. The received signal strength (RSS) measures the energy of the electromagnetic wave. To receive a packet correctly, the received signal strength must be greater than a threshold known as receiver sensitivity. The received signal strength gradually decreases as the distance between the sender and receiver increases. The distance between the sender and receiver can be estimated according to the RSS and propagation model. The estimated distance could be used to detect the attacker with much powerful radio (such as laptop) compared to the radio of the sensor node. On the other hand, the received signal strength should decrease as the system runs since the energy of the sensor node will be consumed. If the received signal strength increases, it is possible that the node identification was stolen by a powerful malicious node.

(c) **Sensing Data Arrival Rate**

There are two types of sensor network applications according to how the sensor nodes are driven to sense data. In the first applications, the sensor nodes are driven by some particular events. In this type of applications, the sensing data will arrive without any pattern. However, in the second applications, the sensor nodes sense the data every preset interval, i.e., driven by the time. In those applications, either missing an expected sensing data or receiving unexpected sensing data identifies some abnormality of the target node.

(d) **RTS Packets Rate**

This feature is calculated on the packets sent from the particular sender, the suspicious node.

(e) **Packet Drop Ratio**

We have stated that a large sensor network usually employs a multi-hop routing protocol to communication since sensor nodes have very limited radio transmission range. Most sensor nodes also work as a route to forward its received packets. A subverted node could attack this forwarding function by dropping packets or selectively forwarding some packets. To calculate this drop ratio, the host node must know the received packets and the forwarded packets of the suspicious node.

(f) **Packet Retransmission Rate**

A packet could be retransmitted when the previous transmission is failed due to conflict. However, such retransmission mechanism could be attacked. A subverted node could retransmit a packet multiple times to exhaust the energy of the receiver or try to alter the aggregation value. Abnormal retransmission rate can be used to detect intrusion.

9.3. Detection Model and Optimization

We would like to use a machine learning algorithm called SLIPPER to build the detection model. The model will be a set of rules. SLIPPER is a confidence-rated boosting algorithm, so each rule learned from its training data set might not have very high prediction accuracy on new data. However, the predictions based on the entire set of rules are expected to be highly true. We had built a detection model using SLIPPER and applied it on KDDCup'99 intrusion detection data set, which was constructed from the raw TCP data for a wired local-area network (LAN) simulating a typical U.S. Air Force LAN. The performance of the detection model on the test data set was better than the winner of the KDDCup'99 classifier contest.

Rules are in IF-THEN form. Most of rules have one or more conjunctive conditions. However, the relationships among rules are not explored and rules in the model are disjunctive in default. Therefore, at least one condition in every rule has to be evaluated on every data to make the final prediction. In wireless sensor network, the CPU has limited computational power and the sensor node has constrained energy, so it is desired to optimize the rule evaluation procedure to reduce unnecessary computation. Each condition consists of a feature name, an operator, and a reference value. For example, "service = telnet", "source_byte <= 147". Some conditions in different rules could have same features. To optimize the detection model, we will explore the relationship among those conditions with same features while ignoring any possible relationship among different features since we assume the features are independent. Among those conditions with the same features, we realize that two kinds of relationships could be used to optimize the rule evaluation procedure. The first relationship is mutually exclusive relationship among conditions such as "service = login" and "service = ftp_data" where these two conditions couldn't be true at the same time. The second relationship is implicit relationship between conditions such as "duration >= 134" and "duration >= 67" where the former implies the latter. For conditions with mutually exclusive relationship, at most only one condition could be true, while all other conditions must be false. So when these conditions are evaluated one by one, as long as the true condition is evaluated, the evaluations on remained conditions with mutually exclusive relationship could be skipped. These conditions with mutually exclusive relationship could be ordered further by its possibility to be true if such information is available. For example, the feature "service" is expected more likely to be "ftp_data" than to be "login", so the condition "service = ftp_data" should be evaluated earlier than condition "service = login". For conditions with implicit relationship, the implied condition ("duration >= 67") should be evaluated only if the implying condition ("duration >= 134") is evaluated to be false.

To utilize these relationships to optimize the condition evaluation, we organize conditions in all rules into a tree structure. Each node consists of a condition to be evaluated and three child trees. The left child tree (true child) will be evaluated when its condition is true, while the right child (false child) tree will be evaluated when its condition is false. Of course, there are some rules such that none of its conditions has mutually exclusive or implicit relationship with any condition in other rules. The middle tree (unconditional child) is built on all conditions from those rules, which will be evaluated before its condition is evaluated. For example, we can organize the four rules listed in Fig. 9.2 into a tree structure shown in Fig. 9.3.

Each node in the tree structure can be described in text mode by a quad (unconditional child, node condition, true child, false child). For example,

R1: IF Service = login   Duration >= 67.
R2: IF Service = ftp_data   Dst_bytes <= 5.
R3: IF Num_access_files >= 1.
R4: IF Duration >= 134   Dst_host_srv_rerror_rate <= 0.

Fig. 9.2.   An example of rule set with four disjunctive rules.

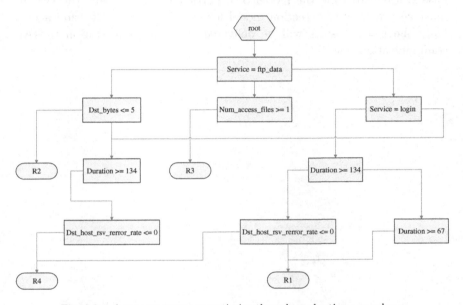

Fig. 9.3.   A tree-structure to optimize the rule evaluation procedure.

the node "Num_access_files >= 1" is saved at (,Num_access_files>=1, R3,). The structure shown in Fig. 9.3 can be stored in text mode as:

   ((, number_access_files >= 1, R3,), service = ftp_data, ((, Duration >= 134 , (, Dst_host_rsv_rerror_rate <= 0, R4,),), Dst_bytes <=5, R2,), (, service = login , (, duration >= 134, (R1, dst_host_rsv_rerror_rate <= 0, R4,), (, Duration >= 67, R1,)), (, Duration >= 134, (, Dst_host_rsv_rerror_rate <= 0, R4,),))).

9.4. Model Tuning

An intrusion detection system will alert possible intrusions, however the alert could be false. The false alerts are also anticipatable in our system.

We have developed a model tuning algorithm [87], which can tune the model (rule's associate confidence) automatically to improve its performance in the future data. The tuning is triggered by the system user after verifying a false alert.

Due to the limited computation power of the sensor node, the model tuning function is separated from the detection agent logically and physically. The model tuner with the system console is resident in the base station. To tune the model of a particular sensor node, the system must keep a copy of detection model for every intrusion detection agent. Only the tuned results will be delivered from the base station to save communication cost.

Chapter 10

Conclusion and Future Research

The work reported in this book mainly aims to the two fundamental problems of an intrusion detection system: the vast quantity and downgrading quality of alarms. As a tool used by the operator, our proposed ADAT IDS can adjust itself to match the operator, rather than the operator adjusts himself/herself to fit it. The hybrid detection model has board detection capability even on new attacks. The model tuning algorithm tunes the detection model automatically to maintain the detection performance. The fuzzy prediction filter makes our system adaptive to the system operator and fuzzy tuning controller gives the operator more powerful but intuitive control in the model tuning procedure. The extension on our system to wireless sensor network is also discussed in this book.

Some future research directions in this area are outlined as follows:

(a) Improve the final arbiter. Our current final arbitral strategies are only based on the binary predictions on one data. The SOMs clustered from the training data could be used to classify the data. It is worthwhile to study how we can integrate the classification result into our final arbiter to improve it.

(b) Incrementally Mine new rules and integrate into the detection model. Those data that no binary classifier makes positive predictions (need to be labeled by the operator) and those data that the current detection model made false predictions (already verified by the operator) could be used to mine new rules.

(c) Improve the fuzzy prediction filter. Our experiment shows that the number of true predictions to the number of false predictions passing the filter is 2 to 1. Compared to the over 90 % overall accuracy on all data sets, current prediction filter is efficient to filter our large number of true predictions. However, an improved prediction filter is beneficial to our system. Is there other factor that could be contributed to the prediction uncertainty? Or is there a better formula to calculate the prediction uncertainty from the current parameters?

(d) Build the extended IDS for wireless sensor network and evaluate its performance. At present, dozens of simulators for wireless sensor network are available. These simulators could be used to build the extended IDS for wireless sensor network.

Cited Literature

1. http://www.cert.org/stats/vulnerability_remediation.html.
2. J. Anderson, *Computer Security Threat Monitoring and Surveillance*, James P. Anderson Co., Fort Washington, PA, 1980.
3. S. Axelsson, "Intrusion Detection System: A Survey and Taxonomy," *Technical Report No. 99-15*, Dept. of Computer Engineering, Chalmers University of Technology, Sweden, Mar. 2000.
4. G. Stoneburner, "Underlying Technical Models for Information Technology Security", NIST (National Institute of Standards and Technology), *Special Publication 800-33*, Dec. 2001.
5. CERT Coordination Center Denial of Service, http://www.cert.org/tech_tips/ denial_of_service.html.
6. T. Sander and C. F. Tschudin, "On the Cryptographic Protection of Mobile Code", *Proceedings of Workshop on Mobile Agents and Security*, Oct. 1997.
7. L. Ma and J. J. P. Tsai, "Formal Verification Techniques for Communication Security Protocols", *Handbook of Software Engineering and Knowledge Engineering*, 2001.
8. R. S. Sandhu and P. Samarati, "Authentication, Access Control, and Intrusion Detection", *The Computer Science and Engineering Handbook*, CRC Press, Boca Raton, FL, 1997.
9. O. Biberstein, D. Buchs, and N. Guelfi, "A Specification Language for Distributed Systems Engineering", *Technical Report 96/167*, Swiss Federal Institute of Technology, Lausanne, 1996.
10. S. Kumar and E. H. Spafford, "A Pattern Matching Model for Misuse Intrusion Detection", *Proceedings of the 17th National Computer Security Conference*, pp. 11–21, Oct. 1994.
11. D. Anderson, T. F. Lunt, H. Javitz, A. Tamaru, and A. Valdes, "Detecting Unusual Program Behavior using the Statistical Component of the Next-Generation Intrusion Detection Expert System (NIDES)", SRI International Computer Science Laboratory, *Technical Report SRI-CSL-95-07*, May 1995.
12. M. Bishop, *Computer Security — Art and Science*, Addison-Wesley, 2002.
13. C. Ko, M. Ruschitzka, and K. Levitt, "Execution Monitoring of Security-Critical Programs in Distributed System: A Specification-Based Approach", *Proceedings of the 1997 IEEE Symposium on Security and Privacy*, pp. 175–187, May 1997.

14. P. Uppuluri and R. Sekar, "Experiences with Specification-Based Intrusion Detection", *Proceedings of Recent Advances in Intrusion Detection (RAID)*, Oct. 2001.

15. Firewall Software White Paper, http://www.firewall-software.com/firewall_faws/types_of_firewall.html.

16. V. Bontchev, "Possible Virus Attacks against Integrity Programs and How to Prevent Them", http://vx.netlux.org/lib/static/vdat/epposatt.htm.

17. N. Ye, X. Li, Q. Chen, S. M. Emran, and M. Xu, "Probabilistic Techniques for Intrusion Detection based on Computer Audit Data", *IEEE Transactions on Systems, Man and Cybernetics*, Part A, Vol. 31, No. 4, pp. 266–274, July 2001.

18. N. Ye, S. M. Emran, Q. Chen, and S. Vilbert, "Multivariate Statistical Analysis of Audit Trails for Host-based Intrusion Detection", *IEEE Transactions on Computers*, Vol. 51, No. 7, pp. 810–820, July 2002.

19. T. Lunt and R. Jagannathan, "A Prototype Real-Time Intrusion-Detection Expert System", *Proceedings of 1988 IEEE Symposium on Security and Privacy*, pp. 59–66, April 1988.

20. T. D. Garvey and T. F. Lunt, "Model based Intrusion Detection", *Proceedings of the 14th National Computer Security Conference*, pp. 372–385, Oct. 1991.

21. K. Ilgun, R. A. Kemmerer, and P. A. Porras, "State Transition Analysis: A Rule-Based Intrusion Detection Approach", *IEEE Transactions on Software Engineering*, Vol. 21, No. 3, pp. 181–199, 1995.

22. H. Debar, M. Becker, and D. Siboni, "A Neural Network Component for an Intrusion Detection System", *Proceedings of 1992 IEEE Symposium on Research in Computer Security and Privacy*, pp. 240–250, May 1992.

23. J. Ryan, M. J. Lin, and R. Miikkulainen, "Intrusion Detection with Neural Networks", *Advances in Neural Information Processing Systems*, Cambridge, MA: MIT Press, 1998.

24. A. Lazarevic, L. Ertoz, V. Kumar, A. Ozgur, and J. Srivastava, "A Comparative Study of Anomaly Detection Schemes in Network Intrusion Detection", *Proceedings of the 3rd SIAM Conference on Data Mining*, May 2003.

25. W. Lee and S. J. Stolfo, "Data Mining Approaches for Intrusion Detection", *Proceedings of the 7th USENIX Security Symposium (SECURITY'98)*, Jan. 1998.

26. W. Lee, S. J. Stolfo, and K. W. Mok, "A Data Mining Framework for Building Intrusion Detection Models", *Proceedings of the 1999 IEEE Symposium on Security and Privacy*, pp. 120–132, 1999.

27. W. Lee, S. J. Stolfo, and P. K. Chan, "Real Time Data Mining-Based Intrusion Detection", *Proceedings of the 2nd DARPA Information Survivability Conference and Exposition (DISCEX II)*, pp. 85–100, June 2001.

28. A. Valdes and K. Skinner, "Probabilistic Alert Correlation", *Proceedings of the 4th International Symposium on Recent Advances in Intrusion Detection*, pp. 54–69, Oct. 2001.

29. P. A. Porras, M. W. Fong, and A. Valdes, "A Mission-Impact-Based Approach to INFOSEC Alarm Correlation", *Proceedings of the 5th International Symposium on Recent Advances in Intrusion Detection (RAID 2002)*, Zurich, Switzerland, pp. 95–114, Oct. 2002.
30. P. Ning, Y. Cui, and D. S. Reeves, "Analyzing Intensive Intrusion Alerts via Correlation", *Proceedings of the 5th International Symposium on Recent Advances in Intrusion Detection (RAID 2002)*, Zurich, Switzerland, pp. 74–94, Oct. 2002.
31. X. Qin and W. Lee, "Statistical Causality Analysis of INFOSEC Alert Data", *Proceedings of the 6th International Symposium, Recent Advances in Intrusion Detection (RAID 2003)*, pp. 73–93, Sep. 2003.
32. B. Morin, L. Me, H. Debar, and M. Ducasse, "M2D2: A Formal Data Model for IDS Alert Correlation", *Proceedings of the 5th International Symposium on Recent Advances in Intrusion Detection (RAID 2002)*, Zurich, Switzerland, pp. 115–137, Oct. 2002.
33. B. Morin and H. Debar, "Correlation of Intrusion Symptoms: An Application of Chronicles", *Proceedings of 6th International Symposium on Recent Advances in Intrusion Detection (RAID 2003)*, pp. 94–112, Sep. 2003.
34. K. Julish and M. Dacier, "Mining Intrusion Detection Alarms for Actionable Knowledge", *Proceedings of the 8th ACM SIGKDD International Conference on Knowledge Discovery and Data Mining*, Edmonton, Canada, pp. 366–375, July 2002.
35. S. Manganaris, M. Christensen, D. Zerkle, and K. Hermiz, "A Data Mining Analysis of RTID Alarms. Computer Networks", *The International Journal of Computer and Telecommunications Networking*, Vol. 34, No. 4, pp. 571–577, 2000.
36. K. Julish, "Mining Alarm Clusters to Improve Alarm Handing Efficiency", *Proceedings of 17th Annual Computer Security Application Conference (ACSAC)*, pp. 12–21, Dec. 2001.
37. C. Kruegel, D. Mutz, W. Robertson, and F. Valeur, "Bayesian Event Classification for Intrusion Detection", *Proceedings of 19th Annual Computer Security Applications Conference (ACSAC 2003)*, pp. 14–23, Dec. 2003.
38. M. Hossian and S. M. Bridges, "A Framework for an Adaptive Intrusion Detection System with Data Mining", *Proceedings of 13th Annual Canadian Information Technology Security Symposium (CITSS 2001)*, Ottawa, Canada, June 2001.
39. T. Kohonen, *Self-Organizing Maps*, 3rd edition, New York: Springer-Verlag LLC, Jan. 2001.
40. kdd.ics.uci.edu/databases/kddcup99/kddcup99.html.
41. K. Tanaka, *An Introduction to Fuzzy Logic for Practical Applications,* 1st edition, Springer-Verlag New York, Inc. Nov. 1996.
42. M. Tubaishat and S. Madria, "Sensor Networks: An Overview", *IEEE Potentials*, Vol. 22, No. 2, pp. 20–23, Apr. 2003.
43. D. E. Denning, "An Intrusion-Detection Model", *IEEE Transactions on Software Engineering*, Vol. SE-13, No. 2, pp. 222–232, Feb. 1987.

44. S. E. Smaha, "Haystack: An Intrusion Detection System", *Proceedings of the IEEE Fourth Aerospace Computer Security Applications Conference*, pp. 37–44, Dec. 1988.

45. Michael M. Sebring, Eric Shellhouse, Mary E. Hanna, and R. Alan Whitehurst, "Expert Systems in Intrusion Detection: A Case Study", *Proceedings of the 11th National Computer Security Conference*, pp. 74–81, Oct. 1988.

46. L. T. Heberlein, G. Dias, K. Levitt, B. Mukherjee, J. Wood, and D. Wolber, "A Network Security Monitor", *Proceedings of the 1990 IEEE Symposium on Research in Security and Privacy*, pp. 296–304, May 1990.

47. J. Hochberg, K. Jackson, C. Stallings, J. F. McClary, D. DuBois, and J. Ford, "NADIR: An Automated System for Detecting Network Intrusion and Misuse", *Computer and Security*, Vol. 12, No. 3, pp. 235–248, May 1993.

48. S. R. Snapp, J. Brentano, G. V. Dias, *et al.*, "DIDS (Distributed Intrusion Detection System) — Motivation, Architecture, and an Early Prototype", *Proceedings of the 14th National Computer Security Conference*, pp. 167–176, Oct. 1991.

49. M. Crosbie and G. Spafford, "Defending a Computer System using Autonomous Agents", *Proceedings of the 18th National Information Systems Security Conference*, Baltimore, Maryland, Oct. 1995.

50. S. Staniford-Chen, S. Cheung, R. Crawford, M. Dilger, J. Frank, J. Hoagland, K. Levitt, C. Wee, R. Yip, and D. Zerkle, "GrIDS — A Graph-Based Intrusion Detection System for Large Networks", *Proceedings of the 19th National Information Systems Security Conference*, Baltimore, MD, Oct. 1996.

51. R. Anderson and A. Khattak, "The Use of Information Retrieval Techniques for Intrusion Detection", *Proceedings of the 1st International Workshop on Recent Advances in Intrusion Detection (RAID'98)*, http://www.raid-symposium.org/raid98. Louvain-la-Neuve, Belgium, Sep. 1998.

52. P. Mell and M. McLarnon, "Mobile Agent Attack Resistant Distributed Hierarchical Intrusion Detection Systems", *Proceedings of the 2nd International Workshop on Recent Advances in Intrusion Detection (RAID 1999)*, http://www.raid-symposium.org/raid99, Sep. 1999.

53. Y. Zhang and W. Lee, "Intrusion Detection in Wireless Ad-hoc Networks", *Proceedings of the 6th Annual International Conference on Mobile Computing and Networking*, pp. 275–283, 2000.

54. A. Agah, S. K. Das, and K. Basu, "Intrusion Detection in Sensor Networks: A Non-cooperative Game Approach", *Proceedings of the 3rd IEEE International Symposium on Network Computing and Applications (NCA'04)*, pp. 343–346, 2004.

55. http://www.ietf.org/html.charters/OLD/idwg-charter.html.

56. http://gost.isi.edu/cidf/.

57. S. Forrest, S. A. Hofmeyr, A. Somayaji, and T. A. Longstaff, "A Sense of Self for UNIX Processes", *Proceedings of the 1996 IEEE Symposium on Research in Security and Privacy*, pp. 120–128, May 1996.

58. P. Kosoresow and S. A. Hofmeyr, "Intrusion Detection via System Call Traces", *IEEE Software*, Vol. 14, No. 5, pp. 35–42, Sep./Oct. 1997.

59. M. Gebski and R. K. Wong, "Intrusion Detection via Analysis and Modeling of User Commands", *Proceedings of the 7th International Data Warehousing and Knowledge Discovery Conference*, Springer-Verlag Berlin, Berlin, LNCS, Vol. 2589, pp. 388–397, 2005.

60. I. T. Jolliffe, *Principal Component Analysis*, Springer-Verlag, 2nd edition, Oct. 2002.

61. Y. Bouzida, F. Cuppens, N. Cuppens-Boulahia, and S. Gombault. "Efficient Intrusion Detection Using Principal Component Analysis", *Proceedings of the 3rd Conference on Security and Network Architectures*, La Londe, France, June 2004.

62. Y. Chen, Y. Li, X. Q. Cheng, and G. Li, "Building Efficient Intrusion Detection Model Based on Principal Component Analysis and C4.5", *Proceedings of International Conference on Communication Technology (ICCT '06)*, Guilin, China, pp. 1–4, Nov. 2006.

63. K. Janson, *Colored Petri Nets: Basic Concepts, Analysis Methods and Practical Use*, Springer-Verlag, 2nd edition, 1996.

64. L. Fausett, *Fundamentals of Neural Networks: Architectures, Algorithms, and Applications*, Prentice-Hall, 1994.

65. P. A. Porras and P. G. Neumann, "EMERALD: Event Monitoring Enabling Responses to Anomalous Live Disturbances", *Proceedings of the 20th National Information Systems Security Conference (NISSC)*, Baltimore, MD, Oct. 1997.

66. G. B. White, E. A. Fisch, and U. W. Pooh. "Cooperating Security Managers: A Peer-Based Intrusion Detection System", *IEEE Network*, Vol. 10, No. 1, pp. 20–23, Jan./Feb. 1996.

67. W. Jansen, P. Mell, T. Karygiannis, and D. Marks, "Mobile Agents in Intrusion Detection and Response", *Proceedings of the 12th Annual Canadian Information Technology Security Symposium*, Ottawa, Canada, June 2000.

68. M. Sabhnani and G. Serpen, "Why Machine Learning Algorithms Fail in Misuse Detection on KDD Intrusion Detection Data Set", *Journal of Intelligent Data Analysis*, Vol. 8, No. 4, pp. 403–415, 2004.

69. M. Sabhnani and G. Serpen, "Application of Machine Learning Algorithms to KDD Intrusion Detection Data set within Misuse Detection Context", *Proceedings of International Conference on Machine Learning: Models, Technologies and Applications*, pp. 209–215, June 2003.

70. M. Sabhnani, Development of An Intrusion Detection System Through Machine Learning and Rule Based Algorithms for Networked Computing, Thesis Presentation in EECS Dept. Univ. of Toledo, Sep. 2002.

71. P. Dokas, L. Ertoz, and V. Kumar, "Data Mining for Network Intrusion Detection", *Proceedings of the NFS Workshop on Next Generation Data Mining*, Nov. 2002.

72. W. Cohen, "Fast Effective Rule Induction", *Proceedings of the 12th International Conference on Machine Learning*, pp. 115–123, July 1995.

73. V. Kumar, "Data Mining for Network Intrusion Detection: Experience with KDD'99 Data Set", *Proceedings of the Workshop on Network Intrusion Detection*, Mar. 2002.
74. G. Giacinto, F. Roli, and L. Didaci, "A Modular Multiple Classifier System for the Detection of Intrusions in Computer Networks", *Proceedings of the 4th International Workshop on Multiple Classifier Systems (MCS 2003)*, pp. 346–355, 2003.
75. R. Agarwal and V. M. Joshi, "PNrule: A New Framework for Learning Classifier Models in Data Mining (A Case-Study in Network Intrusion Detection)", *Proceedings of the 1st SIAM Conference on Data Mining*, pp. 00–15, Apr. 2001.
76. C. Elkan, "Results of the KDD'99 Classifier Learning", *ACM SIGKDD Explorations Newsletter*, Vol. 1, No. 2, pp. 63–64, Jan. 2000.
77. B. Pfahringer, "Winning the KDD99 Classification Cup: Bagged Boosting", *ACM SIGKDD Explorations Newsletter*, Vol. 1, No. 2, pp. 65–66, 2000.
78. I. Levin, "KDD-99 Classifier Learning Contest LLSoft's Results Overview", *ACM SIGKDD Explorations Newsletter*, Vol. 1, No. 2, pp. 67–75, 2000.
79. L. Ertoz, M. Steinbach, and V. Kumar, "Finding Clusters of Different Sizes, Shapes and Densities in Noisy High Dimensional Data", *Proceedings of the 3rd SIAM International Conference on Data Mining*, 2003, http://www.siam.org/meetings/sdm03/proceedings/smd03_05.pdf.
80. D. Y. Yeung and C. Chow, "Parzen-Window Network Intrusion Detectors", *Proceedings of the 6th International Conference on Pattern Recognition*, Vol. 4, pp. 385–388, 2002.
81. J. Gomez and D. Dasgupta, "Evolving Fuzzy Classifiers for Intrusion Detection", *Proceedings of the 2002 IEEE Workshop on Information Assurance*, June 2002.
82. W. Cohen and Y. Singer, "A Simple, Fast, and Effective Rule Learner", *Proceedings of Annual Conference of American Association for Artificial Intelligence*, pp. 335–342, 1999.
83. R. E. Schapire and Y. Singer, "Improved Boosting Algorithms using Confidence-rated Predictions", *Machine Learning*, Vol. 37, No. 3, pp. 297–336, 1999.
84. Z. Yu and J. J. P. Tsai, "A Multi-Class SLIPPER System for Intrusion Detection", *Proceedings of the 28th Annual International Computer Software and Applications Conference (COMPSAC'04)*. Vol. 1, pp. 212–217. Hong Kong, China, Sep. 2004.
85. Z. Yu and J. J. P. Tsai, "An Efficient Intrusion Detection System using a Boosting based Learning Algorithm", *International Journal of Computer Applications in Technology*, Vol. 27, No. 4, pp. 223–231, 2006.
86. I. Dubrawsky and R. Saville, "SAFE: IDS Deployment, Tuning, and Logging in Depth", CISCO SAFE White paper, http://www.cisco.com/go/safe.
87. Z. Yu, J. J. P. Tsai, and T. Weigert, "An Automatically Tuning Intrusion Detection System", *IEEE Transactions on Systems, Man, Cybernetics*, Part B, Vol. 37, No. 2, pp. 373–384, Apr. 2007.
88. M. Mukaidono, *Fuzzy Logic for Beginners*, World Scientific Publishing Co, Pte. Ltd. 2001.

89. X. Wang, *A Course in Fuzzy Systems and Control*, 1st edition. Prentice Hall Prentice, Professional Technical Reference, Aug. 1996.

90. Z. Yu and J. Tsai, "Fuzzy Model Tuning for Intrusion Detection System", *Proceedings of the 3rd International Conference on Autonomic and Trusted Computing*, pp. 193–204, Wu Han, China, Sep. 2006.

91. A. Perrig, R. Szewczyk, V. Wen, D. Culler, and J. D. Tygar, "SPINS: Security Protocols for Sensor Networks", *Wireless Networks*, Vol. 8, No. 5, pp. 521–534, Sep. 2002.

92. S. Zhu, S. Setia, and S. Jajodia, "LEAP: Efficient Security Mechanisms for Large-scale Distributed Sensor Networks", *Proceedings of the 10th ACM Conference on Computer and Communications Security (CCS '03)*, pp. 62–72, Oct. 2003.

93. J. Deng, R. Han, and S. Mishra, "A Performance Evaluation of Intrusion-Tolerant Routing in Wireless Sensor Networks", *Proceedings of the 2nd International IEEE Workshop on Information Processing in Sensor Networks (IPSN'03)*, pp. 349–364, Apr. 2003.

94. J. Undercoffer, S. Avancha, A. Joshi, and J. Pinkston, "Security for Sensor Networks", *Proceedings of CADIP Research Symposium*, 2002.

95. C.Y. Chong and S. P. Kumar, "Sensor Networks: Evolution, Opportunities and Challenges", *Proceedings of the IEEE*, Vol. 91, No. 8, pp. 1247–1256, Aug. 2003.

96. E. Shi and A. Perrig, "Designing Secure Sensor Networks", *IEEE Wireless Communications*, Vol. 11, No. 6, pp. 38–43, Dec. 2004.

97. F. Akyildiz, W. L. Su, Y. Sankarasubramaniam, and E. Cayirci, "A Survey on Sensor Networks", *IEEE Communications Magazine*, Vol. 40, No. 8, pp. 102–114, Aug. 2002.

98. C. Kersey, Z. Yu, and J. J. P. Tsai, "Intrusion Detection for Wireless Network", *Wireless Ad Hoc Networking*, (S. Wu and Y. Tseng, eds.), Auerbach Publications, pp. 505–533, Mar. 2007.

99. Online ATMEGA128L datasheet, http://www.atmel.com/dyn/resources/ prod_ documents/doc2467.pdf.

100. Online datasheet, http://www.xbow.com/Products/Product_pdf_files/ Wireless_pdf/MICA2_Datasheet.pdf.

101. Online datasheet, http://www.xbow.com/Products/Product_pdf_files/ Wireless_pdf/MICAz_Datasheet.pdf.

102. D. Wood and J. A. Stankovic, "Denial of Service in Sensor Networks", *IEEE Computer*, Vol. 35, No. 10, pp. 54–62, Oct. 2002.

103. C. Karlof and D. Wagner, "Secure Routing in Wireless Sensor Networks: Attacks and Countermeasures", *Ad Hoc Networks Journal*, Vol. 1, No. 2–3, pp. 293–315, Elsevier, Sep. 2003.

104. R. Douceur, "The Sybil Attack", *Lecture Notes in Computer Science*, Vol. 2429, pp. 251–260, 2002.

105. Y. C. Hu, A. Perrig, and D. B. Johnson, "Packet Leashes: A Defense against Wormhole Attacks in Wireless Networks", *Proceedings of the 22nd Annual Joint Conference of the IEEE Computer and Communications Societies*, pp. 1976–1986, Mar. 2003.

106. Y. C. Hu, A. Perrig, and D. B. Johnson, "Rushing Attacks and Defense in Wireless Ad Hoc Network Routing Protocols", *Proceedings of the 2nd ACM Workshop on Wireless Security*, pp. 30–40, 2003.

107. B. Przydatek, D. Song, and A. Perrig, "SIA: Secure Information Aggregation in Sensor Networks", *Proceedings of the 1st International Conference on Embedded Networked Sensor Systems*, pp. 255–265, 2003.

108. E. C. H. Ngai, J. Liu, and M. R. Lyu, "On the Intruder Detection for Sinkhole Attack in Wireless Sensor Networks", *Proceedings of IEEE International Conference on Communications (ICC'06)*, Vol. 8, pp. 3383–3389, Istanbul, Turkey, June 2006.

109. R. Roman, J. Zhou, and J. Lopez, "Applying Intrusion Detection Systems to Wireless Sensor Networks", *Proceedings of the 3rd IEEE Consumer Communications and Networking Conference (CCNC 2006)*, Vol. 1, pp. 640–644, Jan. 2006

110. A. P. R. Silva, M. H. T. Martins, B. P. S. Rocha, A. A. F. Loureiro, L. B. Ruiz, and H. C. Wong, "Decentralized Intrusion Detection in Wireless Sensor Networks", *Proceedings of the 1st ACM International Workshop on Quality of Service and Security in Wireless and Mobile Networks*, pp. 16–23, Oct. 2005.

111. W. Heinzelman, A. Chandrakasan, and H. Balakrishnan, "Energy-Efficient Communication Protocols for Wireless Microsensor Networks", *Proceedings of the 33rd Annual Hawaii International Conference on Systems Sciences*, Jan. 2000.

112. A. Woo and D. E. Culler, "A Transmission Control Scheme for Media Access in Sensor Networks", *Proceedings of the ACM/IEEE International Conference on Mobile Computing and Networking*, pp. 221–235. Rome, Italy, July 2001.

113. Z. Yu, J. J. P. Tsai, and T. Weigert, "An Adaptive Automatically Tuning Intrusion Detection System", *ACM Transactions on Autonomous and Adaptive Systems*, Vol. 3, No. 3, July 2008.

114. D. Zhang and J. J. P. Tsai, *Machine Learning Applications in Software Engineering*, World Scientific Inc., 2005.

115. D. Zhang and J. J. P. Tsai, *Advances in Machine Learning Applications in Software Engineering*, IGI Publishing Inc., PA, 2007.

116. J. J. P. Tsai and P. S. Yu, *Machine Learning in Cyber Trust: Security, Privacy, Reliability*, Springer, New York, 2009.

117. L. Ma and J. J. P. Tsai, *Security Modeling and Analysis of Mobile Agent Systems*, Imperial College Press, London, 2006.

118. Z. Yu and J. J. P. Tsai, "A Framework of Machine Learning based Intrusion Detection for Wireless Sensor Networks", *Proceedings of the 2nd IEEE International Conference on Sensor Network, Ubiquitous, and Trustworthy Computing (SUTC2008)*, pp. 272–393, June 11–13, 2008.

119. W. Cui, R. H. Katz, and W. Tan, "Binder: An Extrusion-Based Break-In Detector for Personal Computers", *Proceedings of 2005 USENIX Annual Technical Conference*, Apr. 2005.

120. Y. Luo and J. J. P. Tsai, "A Framework for Extrusion Detection Using Machine Learning", *Proceedings of the 11th IEEE Symposium on Object/Component/Service-Oriented Real-Time Distributed Computing (ISORC08)*, May 5–7, 2008.

121. W. Lee and S. Stolfo, "A Framework for Constructing Features and Models for Intrusion Detection Systems", *ACM Transactions on Information and System Security*, Vol. 3, No. 4, Nov. 2000.

122. L. A. Zadeh, "Fuzzy Sets", *Information and Control*, Vol. 8, No. 3, pp. 338–353, June 1965.

123. V. Devarashetty, J. J. P. Tsai, L. Ma, and D. Zhang, "Modeling of Secure Sensor Networks Using an Extended Elementary Object System", *Proceedings of the 7th IEEE International Conference on Cognitive Informatics*, Stanford University, CA, Aug. 14–16, 2008.

Index

169